Praise for *Selling Your Value Proposition*

'We are living in the Age of the Customer. *Selling Your Value Proposition* provides leaders with fresh, insightful advice on how to drive the customer-centric business transformation our new world requires. The time has come for every employee to join the sales team, and Barnes, Blake and Howard provide a blueprint with powerful case studies to arm leaders with what they need to get started. A must-read for the transformational leader of the future.' **Cate Gutowski, VP, Commercial Digital Thread, GE Digital**

'In *Creating and Delivering Your Value Proposition* the Futurecurve team helped companies tackle the central, most critical, question they need to address in order to be successful in the market: what is it that makes us unique? Put differently, why should your customers buy from you instead of your competitors? Now, in this terrific follow-up book, they help companies translate their unique value proposition into a set of messages that the salesforce can use to drive growth. In so doing, the authors tackle a question that is just as difficult and vexing for managers: what would have to be true in the customer's world for them to want to PAY us for our unique differentiators? Together, these two books – packed with practical advice, tools and case examples – are must-read material for B2B CEOs, sales leaders and marketers intent on driving growth in markets increasingly crowded with seemingly commoditized offerings.' **Matthew Dixon, Group Leader, CEB, and co-author,** *The Challenger Sale* **and** *The Challenger Customer*

'Packed with tried and tested tactics and dozens of examples from real organizations, this is an essential read for executives in large corporates or anyone who wants to be customer-centric (internal or external), innovate and stay ahead of the game.' **Simon Gale, Procurement Director, Sony Europe**

'If we keep looking at our customers through the same lens, having the same conversations with them, telling them the same things, not properly hearing the answers, we wake up one day and we don't understand each other any more – and worse, we have been replaced. This book wakes us up and gives us a new way to look at and think about our customers, and then transform the relationships that we have with them.' **Andy Head, Business Development Director, NATS**

'Deconstructing all the key elements of what a genuine customer-centric organization looks like, Barnes, Blake and Howard guide us through the most engaging examination of value, and its relationship with customers and organizations. With an emphasis on how to use the tools and implement them effectively, the authors deliver a must-read for all executives seeking to gain, or further, their organization's advantage through deep and resilient relationships with customers.' **Christopher Taylor, Executive Vice President – Strategic Development, Survitec**

'This book is essentially the most helpful business mentor you've ever met. It thoughtfully reminds us that it's our customers' lives and ambitions that govern their appetite for our products and services, not our predetermined sales plan. As a leader from local government, where customers and sales are not familiar concepts, I found its clear, concise and creative insights and methods empowering. First to understand where our products and services sit with helping our customers have a better day, on their terms not ours. Then with that humility and integrity to execute a sales process that unlocks our customers' own fulfilment. I think we all want to buy from businesses who can do that with grace and style.' **Andrew Grant, Chief Executive, Aylesbury Vale District Council**

'*Selling Your Value Proposition* provides insight, acumen and a clear understanding of how to effect organizational change – without turning the organization and its processes upside down. The case-study approach is most helpful, not only to provide exemplars but to show that the challenges in business today are not simply based on the size of the business, but on system-level and individual-level factors that are driving both internal staff behaviour and also customer behaviour. Being able to respond to these sometimes competing forces in a strategic and tactical way is critical for growth and acceleration.' **Dr Femida Gwadry-Sridhar, founder and CEO, Pulse Infoframe Inc**

'A critically important survival manual for a digital, disruptive age, in which your value proposition must continually evolve to keep up with connected customers.'
Dave Gray, founder, XPLANE, and author, *The Connected Company*

'*Selling Your Value Proposition* isn't only about your value proposition. It's about aligning everything your company does to put the customer at the centre of everything you do. The book focuses on learning what value experiences your customers and markets expect, then on mobilizing your delivery of those experiences through sharp sales and marketing execution. *Selling Your Value Proposition* helps you align everything you do to create value experiences that are meaningful to your customers.' **Dave Brock, CEO, Partners In EXCELLENCE**

'This book shows senior executives how to develop authentic and systemic value propositions in a world where both technology and societal awareness are changing how and why people choose to buy. The authors provide clear guidance on how to implement genuine change through their proven methodology and 10 laws of value proposition selling. I recommend this book to both established businesses and the new generation of entrepreneurs who wish to create genuinely engaging companies in which the whole organization is totally focused on understanding and meeting customer needs.' **Simon Robinson, co-author, *Customer Experiences with Soul: A new era in design* and *Holonomics***

'Your value proposition is at the heart of everything you need to do to sell and grow effectively. Yet my experience is that the vast majority of companies fail to invest enough time and energy into this key area. In this superb book, Cindy Barnes, Helen Blake and Tamara Howard bring their expertise and experience alive with a clear road map to enable you to put together a powerful value proposition, translate it into a selling proposition and ultimately transform your business into an authentic, trusted "selling organization". If you are ambitious to win more business and grow your sales faster, this book is a must-read.'
Gordon McAlpine, entrepreneur, mentor, and bestselling author, *Scale Up Millionaire*

Selling Your Value Proposition

How to transform your business into a selling organization

Cindy Barnes
Helen Blake
Tamara Howard

KoganPage

Publisher's note

Every possible effort has been made to ensure that the information contained in this book is accurate at the time of going to press, and the publisher and authors cannot accept responsibility for any errors or omissions, however caused. No responsibility for loss or damage occasioned to any person acting, or refraining from action, as a result of the material in this publication can be accepted by the editor, the publisher or any of the authors.

First published in Great Britain and the United States in 2017 by Kogan Page Limited

2nd Floor, 45 Gee Street	c/o Martin P Hill Consulting	4737/23 Ansari Road
London	122 W 27th St, 10th Floor	Daryaganj
EC1V 3RS	New York, NY 10001	New Delhi 110002
United Kingdom	USA	India

www.koganpage.com

ISBN   978 0 7494 7991 6
E-ISBN   978 0 7494 7992 3

British Library Cataloguing-in-Publication Data

A CIP record for this book is available from the British Library.

Library of Congress Cataloging-in-Publication Data

Names: Barnes, Cindy, 1961- author. | Blake, Helen, 1962- author. | Howard, Tamara, author.
Title: Selling your value proposition : how to transform your business into a selling organization / Cindy Barnes, Helen Blake, Tamara Howard.
Description: London ; New York : Kogan Page, 2017. | Includes bibliographical references and index.
Identifiers: LCCN 2017014417 (print) | LCCN 2017004825 (ebook) | ISBN 9780749479923 (ebook) | ISBN 9780749479916 (alk. paper)
Subjects: LCSH: Customer relations. | Value. | Selling. | Organizational change.
Classification: LCC HF5415.5 (print) | LCC HF5415.5 .B368233 2017 (ebook) | DDC 658.85–dc23

Typeset by Integra Software Services, Pondicherry
Print production managed by Jellyfish
Printed and bound by CPI Group (UK) Ltd, Croydon, CR0 4YY

CONTENTS

08   Creating the selling organization 171

With gratitude to all our family and friends who have supported us unswervingly throughout our lives and careers. Cindy, Helen and Tamara

LIST OF CONTRIBUTORS

Our thanks to:
Ian Bolger, Bolgers
Dave Brock, Partners in EXCELLENCE
Peter Cook, Human Dynamics
Darin De Stefano, writer
Matt Dixon, Corporate Executive Board
Dave Gray, XPLANE
Giles Hutchins, Future Fit Leadership Academy
Dominic John, Customer Alignment
Gene Leonard, LBS Partners
Simon Robinson, Holonomics Education

Our case study contributors:
Jim Bergin, Glanbia Ingredients Ireland
Phil Blades, Aircom International
Andrew Boland, NVD
Tom Cafferkey, LotusWorks
Andy Donlan, Thermodial
Robert Dunne, GlycoSelect
Sean Finlay and Andrew Gaynor, Geoscience Ireland
Paul Foley, DreamTec Software
Andrew Grant, Aylesbury Vale District Council
Andy Head, NATS
Dr Karl McCarthy, Biocel Ltd
Paul McDonald, Sonitus Systems
Jonathan Reed, Mergermarket Group
Paul Roberts, New Oxford Advisory and Consulting
Barry Smith, Abcon Industrial Products Ltd
Lucia Valente, Computational Class Notes

FOREWORD

The company is now fully prepared for the past.

This statement is my rephrasing of 'The army is now fully prepared for the previous war', inspired by John Gall, in his reference to historian Arnold Toynbee, in which he explains how armies are typically 'one war behind' or one battle behind in terms of strategy, tactics and technology.

This thinking is very relevant to our organizational world today. Most of today's organizations are now fully prepared for the past – past market conditions, past business challenges and past opportunities. How many times do we find ourselves rethinking, redoing, restructuring, reshuffling, reskilling and re-everything – as if the reality had just stopped for us? Hi there! I am going to stop time so that you can catch up. Look at all the benchmarking data, all the trend reports, all the rankings of the Most Admired, the Most Followed and the Most Sainted of companies, do your re-something, and then, Me, God of Time, will push the button again.

Really?

Many revamps of product development involve the refining of the machine, the addition of better oil and the change of a few pieces here and there. Not many look at a new product development that may break the rules and jump the curve.

Many human resources/organization development (HR/OD) people, practices and processes still try to reskill and hire for skills based on an old skill set that worked in the past. Not many are courageous enough to look at what may be needed for the future, including people with zero experience in the relevant area of expertise.

Many consulting approaches are still aimed at providing comfort to the client (and the consultants' bank managers) as opposed to providing challenge, which is much more inconvenient and stressful but is vital to the forward-looking organization.

Marketing and selling processes are often still using old toolkits created in a time when business was more linear and predictable and that are inappropriate to new products and market positioning.

Yes, much of what people do in organizations is to get the company fully prepared for the past.

The whole area of value proposition, from design to implementation and selling needs is to be looked at properly, making sure that a business creates a whole system that will elegantly prepare it for the future, and not the past.

Cindy, Helen and Tamara unpack this challenge with passion and skill as professionals who have been at this forefront for a long time. Their contribution is significant for the future, not the last war.

Dr Leandro Herrero
Chief Organization Architect
The Chalfont Project/Viral Change

ACKNOWLEDGEMENTS

In this world of change, the importance of customer value must not be underestimated or understated. For sales professionals and other senior executives in companies of all sizes around the world, harnessing authentic customer value into value propositions which inform sales propositions is a powerful way of generating better business.

Our influencers include all our customers, clients and colleagues who, over the years, have helped to shape and refine our work.

We here express our appreciation to those who supported us, worked with us daily, and helped bring this book to fruition.

First, extensive thanks must go to Mary Pasby for bringing her years of experience in marketing, sales and research to bear on our work. We could not have brought this book to fruition without her.

Paul Waddington was our amazing, patient wordsmith – we're indebted, Paul.

Suzi McGhee prepared, corrected and co-ordinated the manuscript and illustrations. Our thanks go to her for her continual diligence and perseverance.

Darin De Stefano was our tireless proofreader and insightful copy editor. Our thanks to him for his patience and tenacity.

Other acknowledgements go to: Alison Carter, Lucy Cooper, Jane Tennant, Ostii Ananda, Lynn Serafinn, Catherine Martin, Leandro Herrero, Paul Roberts and Professor Jonathan Smith.

Final acknowledgements go to wonderful social media contacts and friends – some of whom we know and some we have never met but each person has been invaluable with their knowledge, help and support, including: Mike Parker, Neelesh Marik, Rmala d'Aalam, Charles O'Malley, Laura Martinez Galera, Patrick Andrews, Floris Koot, John Kellden, Keith Gould, Nadine Hack and Jan Höglund.

Introduction

There is a paradox in business today. Customers have more power than ever, yet they are less satisfied with the businesses that serve them. The result is that many businesses, particularly those that are well established, are losing out to disruptive new competitors.

In our first book, *Creating and Delivering Your Value Proposition* (Barnes, Blake and Pinder, 2009), we explored how businesses can reconnect with their customers by creating a better customer experience. There are now 600 implementations of Futurecurve's Value Proposition Builder™ methodology in organizations around the world. We have been able to observe it in action as companies use it to tackle their own particular challenges. What we have seen has shown that it is a powerful tool for restructuring and repairing customer relationships. However, its output alone is often not enough. To really reap the rewards of value proposition work, companies need to make more profound changes to the way they work and act. Businesses have had varied degrees of success in doing this. In this book, we explore their stories.

In particular, we look at one of the key areas where businesses need to make adjustments: their sales approach. Unless this is modified to take advantage of a company's value proposition, many of the benefits are lost. This is crucial because, without sales, there is no business.

So why now? What is creating this paradox in modern business?

Many forces have converged to change the face of commerce in recent years. Driven by technology and the relaxation of trade barriers, many large companies have become globalized. During this process, the customer has often been left behind – turned into little more than a number on a balance sheet. This trend holds true for business-to-business as well as consumer sales organizations.

Success, ethics and the millennials

Today, there is a rise in ethical business and business practices, spurred in part by the demands of millennials: those born between 1980 and 1999. This generation has grown up with technology and is more questioning of business. Millennials use social media and other peer-to-peer systems to filter out truth from spin. Twitter, for example, creates a community and a sense of power against big business and bad practice. This age group – which of course comprises potential customers and employees – can quickly and easily find a different supplier or employer.

Making the change

How do companies change to meet the challenges of globalization and empowered, demanding customers? Realizing that they are not mechanical entities but collections of people is an important step. As the world becomes more interconnected and people become more interdependent on each other, psychological insights will play a growing role in helping people to understand and navigate the complex interactions played out daily between employees, customers and all stakeholders. These insights are a huge part of the value proposition approach explored in this book.

The approach we advocate is not about fixing one or two parts of the business: it is a systemic view that examines all key aspects of the business together. Experience shows that it is never just one thing that is broken. When most companies try to fix the problem, the solutions often involve uncoordinated activities that focus on rational factors at the expense of the emotional and psychological. As a result, their efforts fail to halt the business decline.

This failure occurs because they reach what we term The Solution Gap. This phrase describes a disconnection between how a salesperson sees what they are selling, how the customer sees it, what they want to buy and how the business supports the sales process. The Solution Gap can only be bridged using a joined-up approach that encompasses the whole business and its wider stakeholders, especially its customers.

Businesses need to integrate the customer into their core business processes if they want to solve this problem. Selecting and implementing the best marketing strategy and sales approach is key to achieving this objective. That is why this book will focus on these business areas. It will show how the Value Proposition Builder™ approach can be extended to have a long-term, transformational impact on sales, marketing and the whole business.

Many companies have successfully achieved this holistic approach. However, others have implemented value proposition designs by only changing one aspect of their business, without considering the consequences for the whole organization. Often, they focus on short-term gain rather than more systemic, longer-term objectives.

Examples of business demise due to short-termism illustrate what can happen. Remember Blockbuster or, less well known in Europe, the Joseph Schlitz Brewing Company? Much has been written about Blockbuster's failure as a result of new market disruptors such as Netflix. However, its demise was heavily influenced by the business tactic of focusing on only one or two key areas to increase revenue, notably the charging of late payment fines to customers. This tactical approach left the business blindsided by technological innovations and new competitors. In the case of Schlitz, the challenges of meeting large-volume demands while also cutting the cost of production led it to take shortcuts in the brewing process, which alienated its traditional customers. Ultimately, it was sold to a rival. In this instance, Schlitz ignored what its customers wanted – in the interest of satisfying increasing sales and reducing costs – and in doing so it lost the whole business.

The business press dissects the corpses of failed businesses to understand what can be learned from them. Harder to find are those companies that do play the long game, approaching their businesses in a systemic way and considering all the areas of change that need to be tackled. Unilever is a prime example of a company that acts systematically in all of its businesses, across all of its brands and supply chain, with a goal of making sustainable living commonplace. This behaviour is evident in projects such as The Foundry, a global crowdsourcing platform that looks to solve sustainability issues in the areas of sanitation, hygiene and nutrition (The Foundry, 2016). The core belief that runs like a golden thread throughout Unilever is that it cannot have a healthy business in an unhealthy society. Best-selling author and thought leader Simon Robinson describes sustainability as 'the quality of an organization's relationship with all stakeholders', where those stakeholders are internal, customers, value chain, nature and the individual (Robinson and Moraes Robinson, 2014). This view supports the systemic approach detailed in the pages that follow.

Authenticity, this book and its readers

This book focuses on selling ethically, authentically and successfully. Today we are seeing the growth of ethically driven companies whose values are authentic and underpin their business processes. Throughout the book, all recommendations will steer readers towards developing an authentic business. As part of this process, one important point must be addressed: what is authentic selling? Is it helping customers or manipulating them? In an authentic business, sales tools and techniques are used to help customers. When they sell ethically, the business and its sales staff work with customers to help them shape solutions and offerings that are of genuine value to the customer. In this way, the ethical selling process becomes a win/win situation.

In the groundbreaking book *Holonomics* (Robinson and Moraes Robinson, 2014) Simon and Maria Robinson argue that people in business must adopt a 'holonomic' way of thinking, a dynamic and authentic understanding of the relationships within a business system, and an appreciation of the whole.

So, who should read this book?

This book is aimed at traditional businesses, new businesses and entrepreneurs that want to (re)connect to their customers and provide products and services of genuine value to them. To implement this change successfully, the reader will most likely be a senior executive running an entire company, division or large department.

Any business that sets off on this journey and stays with it will ultimately find itself with happier, more engaged customers and employees; solid revenues; a sense of business community; and a successful sales process. Management – indeed, the whole company – will feel confident. Everyone in the business will know what they are doing, why they are doing it and how this contributes to the customer experience.

However, creating this integrated approach requires special tools and techniques. The Value Proposition Builder™ framework uses a psychology-based approach (a mix of transactional analysis and phenomenology) to conduct stakeholder interviews. This uncovers unique rational and emotional insights, enabling businesses to address both these dimensions when they change how they work, leading to innovative breakthroughs and integrated processes.

Leading sales expert Dave Brock says: 'To be truly customer-centric you need to talk in the customer's language and from their perspective. So you wouldn't talk about the offerings that you want to sell, rather you would talk about the customer problems that you are going to solve. You wouldn't talk about the sales process; you would talk about the customer buying process.' We agree wholeheartedly with Brock. But in this book we are talking primarily to companies that sell, rather than to their customers, so to avoid confusion and for the purpose of simplicity we are going to stick with 'company-focused' language. For this reason we talk about 'sales proposition' rather than 'buying proposition' throughout.

Get ready to read

This book begins by examining the current business climate and how the market has changed forever (Chapter 1). It looks at some of the symptoms of this market shift and how various companies have responded. The world has changed over the past decade and continues to change – businesses ignore this shift at their peril.

Chapter 2 explains why value propositions are central to navigating these changes, and how they form the foundation for effective sales propositions and stories.

In Chapter 3, we cover how to design a value proposition. Does the business approach align with what it is that customers value?

If not, what does 'good' look like? When a business is not aligned (and many are not), business leaders feel desperate and impotent. In large businesses, making the necessary changes is like turning around a large oil tanker: slow and time-consuming. Sometimes, it is difficult to know where to begin. The Value Proposition Builder™ emphasizes the importance of customer and market research that treats the customer as someone within, not outside, the organization's boundary. Businesses work *with* the customer; they are not doing things *to* them or *for* them. For many companies, this needs a mental and behavioural shift. In this chapter, we introduce a case study that will be used throughout the book to provide a real example of how a company can move through the whole process of embedding their value proposition into the way it works.

Chapter 4 explains how to translate the value proposition into a sales proposition. There are two components to 'value proposition selling': the first is the actual product, service or offering being sold, while the second focuses on 'how to sell' or 'the sales process'. There are many misconceptions about selling: often, companies see it as a single discipline. In fact, there are a range of sales approaches, each requiring different skills, processes and support from the business. For the best results, a business should understand what it sells and then select the best sales approach.

The Value Pyramid™ can be used to map customer buying behaviours for any business against its offerings and help to identify any adjustments that the organization needs to make. The customer's understanding of a business's offering will be informed by how the offerings have been positioned on the Value Pyramid™. For example, it can help to select the optimal selling style for the business, such as transactional or consultative.

Businesses need to change the way they support this type of selling. In fact, as Dave Brock suggests, they may even need to change the people who do the selling. 'Our customers don't need salespeople calling on them. They need business people who sell' (Brock, 2016). Finally, any company that wants to move up the Value Pyramid™ needs to ensure that all these changes are embedded in the business.

Chapter 5 reviews sales approaches and the sales process, with a particular focus on how the customer feels at each stage. Two elements – the rational and emotional – play a key role in helping a business to design an effective sales strategy and select the most effective sales approach and style.

Chapter 6 focuses on 'the sales story'. Storytelling is an integral part of sales proposition communication for a number of reasons. It connects listeners to the storyteller emotionally and this bond plays a key role in the sales process. Well-documented research demonstrates that storytelling often provides critical engagement between sales staff and prospective clients. From this research, we know that unique physiological responses occur in the brain when relating to stories. Mirror neurons contribute to coherence between a speaker's presentation and the receptivity of his/her audience. The speaker and listener together establish a shared context involving various degrees of neural coupling. This process results in senses of shared perspective and empathy between the salesperson and the buyer.

In Chapter 7 we summarize the 10 Laws of Value Proposition Selling:

- Law 1: the whole company plays a role in supporting the sales process.
- Law 2: the customer is part of the business system.
- Law 3: the structures and behaviours of a business must be kept in balance with each other.
- Law 4: sales behaviours must be directed towards helping the customer gain maximum value from sales offerings.
- Law 5: understand and be clear about the difference between marketing and selling.
- Law 6: ensure that all business processes support the market positioning.
- Law 7: don't try to change everything all at once; you need an evolutionary plan.
- Law 8: use the sales process as a guide and select the appropriate sales approach and style for your market positioning.
- Law 9: you can't mix your selling styles in one meeting.
- Law 10: this process – the value proposition work and organizational adjustments – never stops.

These are the foundations upon which this book is based. If a business genuinely wants to offer value to its customers, these laws provide an excellent checklist to assess how the business is aligned with this aspiration.

Finally, Chapter 8 explores how organizations have changed their structures to support value proposition selling. We use case studies to illustrate how starting with psychology-based research and the Value Proposition Builder™, companies have gone on to restructure their businesses so that marketing and sales efforts are precisely calibrated to their customers.

References

Barnes, Cindy, Blake, Helen and Pinder, David (2009) *Creating and Delivering Your Value Proposition*, Kogan Page, London

Brock, Dave (2016) [accessed 7 June 2016] Business People Who Sell [Blog] Partners In EXCELLENCE, 11 March [Online] http://partnersinexcellenceblog.com/business-people-who-sell/

Robinson, Simon and Moraes Robinson, Maria (2014) *Holonomics: Business where people and planet matter*, Floris Books, Edinburgh

The Foundry [accessed 9 November 2016] *Unilever*. © 2016 [Online] https://foundry.unilever.com/

How the world has changed   01

Why should a business change anything? If it is big, successful, has a good track record and is a well-known brand in its marketplace, why fix what does not appear to be broken? The short answer is: because the world is changing.

First, people are getting richer. 'We are reaching a tipping point, where over the next several years the global middle class will expand dramatically. This is one of the most important features of today's global economic landscape' (Kharas, 2011). Why is this important? Because the richer people are, the more they want differentiation in products and services.

India and China have the fastest-growing middle classes. China is on the verge of becoming a middle-class nation. By 2030 over 70 per cent of China's population could be middle class, consuming nearly US $10 trillion in goods and services. These individuals have an enormous impact on the global marketplace. In 2013, the Chinese bought more new Rolls-Royce cars than any other nation. Since then the Chinese economy has been hit and this growth is declining, but China is still Rolls-Royce's fourth-biggest global market after the United States, the Middle East and Europe (Kharas, 2011).

Second, there are more people on the planet. On the one hand, this growth means there are more consumers for companies' products and services. On the other, there are also more people competing for the same natural resources – water, power and raw materials. Everything manufactured ultimately originates from natural resources, which are finite. Yet many businesses and individuals behave as though resources are infinite. These behaviours are unsustainable. As humankind degrades the planet and extracts more resources, our ecologies become dangerously unbalanced and approach a point of no return. There will be more and more commercial consequences around this issue as time progresses.

As scarcity increases, so does cost. At some point, the resources upon which everyone depends will be more expensive or simply no longer available. Governments are trying to tackle these problems but cannot do so alone. They need the help and the co-operation of businesses and consumers. Companies need to be prepared to protect those resources to ensure they remain plentiful, or find alternative sources. Successful companies will do both and, more and more, consumers will demand it. Various global surveys are showing that millennials (born circa 1980–99) support sustainability actions. Millennials are fast becoming a powerful commercial voice as they move into middle age and can afford to pay to support their ethical stance.

Finally, businesses are changing. Some international companies have grown larger than their home country. Growing beyond continental borders, they are now truly global forces. Economically, these organizations can influence local economies and wield as much power as some governments. In fact, the largest businesses have higher revenues than many countries and their economic power and influence is greater than all but the largest countries. For example, at the end of 2015, Wal-Mart's revenues matched the gross domestic product (GDP) of Poland.

How did this shift of economic power happen?

Deregulation and the easing of trade barriers between countries has enabled much of this business growth. Thanks to technology and the globalization and deregulation of financial services, the costs associated with international trade have fallen: the formation of the European Union (EU) has helped speed up the process within Europe, while the growth of processing power and cloud computing have enabled ways of working that make physical location less relevant to employees and customers alike.

This new paradigm has changed the way businesses behave. For more and more businesses the focus has shifted to short-term returns and bottom-line numbers, and in most cases, to the detriment of other 'stakeholders' in the business. Traditionally, a business served its customers and many also tried to make a positive impact on their communities and employees. Of course, all companies also needed to 'serve' their investors, but tried to do so in a balanced way so that all stakeholders are served.

CASE STUDY

National Vehicle Distribution (NVD) is an automotive transportation and logistics company based in Ireland. Its customers include manufacturers and dealers in many countries. In an effort to drive down costs, automotive manufacturers have implemented highly regimented purchasing processes, driving ever downward the amount their supply chain can charge. For example, in order to achieve the 'best price' per activity, many manufacturers send out separate tenders for each stage of the delivery process: transporting from factory to port; ship transport; customs clearance; delivery and storage at an intermediate destination plus repair to any damaged goods; and finally, delivery to dealer. But is this the best approach?

Although the apparent 'cost' at each step has been forced down, these manufacturers have created other costs and issues by working this way. Different companies perform each step in the delivery of new cars to dealers, so it is difficult to follow any car on its journey or know where or which company might have caused damage during the transport. In later chapters, we will go on to explore how NVD has dealt with the challenges of a marketplace in which its large customers now have a 'broken' procurement process that does not support the changing needs of their businesses.

NVD's large customers had reached an impasse. Prices had reached rock bottom, so there were little or no further savings to be made from a cost-obsessed logistics model. However there were great benefits to be gained if the various steps could be joined up. Unfortunately, in most countries, each step was being managed by many different, often small businesses that were not in a position to link up. Furthermore, a 'logistics solution' to solve this problem could not be purchased using the traditional procurement processes.

Many businesses will need to learn how to change the way they buy such a solution – the automotive industry is just a well-documented example. Other large businesses face similar issues. These companies have painted themselves into a corner. Change must come from within so that they have a mechanism to procure appropriately, by focusing on 'value' to the business rather than cost.

I'm not a commodity, I'm an individual

Today, in many large corporations, employees have become more commoditized – treated as numbers with a high churn. Companies worry less about the loss of any one individual as long as the overall numbers are met. As long as the company's buying targets are met and staff numbers are adequate, then executives tend to be satisfied. This attitude has set the scene for a major change in employee attitudes and loyalty. The Edelman 2015 State of Employee Engagement study (Snyder, 2015) showed that:

- Employee engagement is still widely perceived as falling under the domain of 'HR issues' versus being a driver of business performance. Almost 50 per cent of organizations fail to measure employees' engagement with the customer or the brand.

- There is a distinct lack of strategy, with only 55 per cent of organizations having an explicit employee engagement strategy. Among those that do have a strategy, 86 per cent of senior leaders are familiar with it and only 65 per cent of people managers and 38 per cent of employees are aware of it.

- Engagement is hugely overreported. Half of respondents reported engagement scores above 70 per cent in recent surveys; however, many rely on generic questions that are easy to answer positively versus more discerning, tailored questions that drive action planning and change.

- Organizations do not consistently act on engagement survey data. Only slightly more than half the companies studied say employees believe senior leaders will listen to their opinions and even fewer (42 per cent) believe that positive change will happen as a result.

- Leadership behaviours and communications effectiveness are the two areas that organizations are focusing on to improve engagement (74 per cent and 70 per cent, respectively).

Today, more and more employees are cynical and distrusting, and question why they should be loyal to a brand or business that does not care about them. There is a direct correlation between happy employees and happy customers.

Customers feel commoditized too. In the name of cost reduction, many businesses (and governments) have streamlined their organizational process to maximize efficiency, but in doing so have cut off much human-to-human contact. Phones are answered by computerized systems that ask the customer to do all the work once done by a customer service department: 'Press 1 if you want to buy something, press 2 for service management…' Not all customer issues are merely 'transactional' activities like this, which (eventually) solve a problem. Unhappy customers, frustrated customers and angry customers all need to feel they are being listened to by another human being. Will people be loyal to a machine? Both customers and employees feel disempowered and at the mercy of the system as there is no one to listen to complaints or respond to non-standard issues. There is no human connection.

Do businesses care?

This is a good question. Many businesses espouse values that 'put the customer first' but then enact behaviours and systems that do not support these values. While many call centres do use real people to make contact, often the discussions are so scripted that the call-centre staff can actually do very little. The responsibility given to people working in these types of call centres is so limited that a customer might as well be speaking to a machine. The scripts used by the staff take away their ability to be human. They remove the relationship and the two-way intimacy of genuine human engagement. As many of us will have experienced, this situation can lead to strong negative emotions: while the transaction may ultimately have been successful, the experience was poor.

Does this bad feeling really impact the bottom line? The short answer is: not immediately, but yes, eventually it does. More importantly, the same technology and business setting that has enabled these efficiencies and disenfranchised customers has opened the door to innovative, new market entrants and 'disruptors'. These new businesses pose another threat to the apparently successful, large business.

With the internet of things (IoT), companies can evolve from product businesses to service businesses that are capable of effecting real economic and social change. The issue for established companies, however, is not merely being able to change what they do by moving to digitally enabled products and services – there is a huge behavioural change needed with existing staff, and the key front-line customer interface of those staff is the salespeople.

The best-known examples of these new innovators are Netflix, Airbnb and Uber. The latter two use technology to act as a platform to bring together suppliers and potential customers. In the case of Uber, individual car owners become taxi drivers, providing a reliable and more cost-effective service than many traditional taxi businesses can provide. Airbnb offers homeowners the ability to rent out their rooms or whole residences to individuals seeking accommodation. Airbnb acts like a travel agent for clean, inexpensive hotel rooms at a much lower cost than traditional hotels. Each of these businesses uses technology to facilitate a peer-to-peer (P2P) connection between customer and supplier.

This P2P business model puts people in touch with other people who would otherwise never have found each other, and the business takes a payment for these services. While Airbnb and Uber targeted mainstream customers, Netflix initially targeted customers who were early adopters with niche interests. Its strategy was to grow the business out from this targeted elite. Then, when the infrastructure was ready to support a wider audience, a shift occured when the rise of streaming video enabled Netflix to capture the much larger mainstream market.

Today even large, traditional businesses are beginning to look over their shoulders. Executives ask: 'Is there a disruptor in my business sector? How can we defend ourselves?' The short answer is: provided your business has happy customers, most will not leave you. But, give them a reason to shift... And the reality is that most businesses are not adapting well. The short-term focus on bottom-line results typically means that in an attempt to maintain profits they employ tactical efforts such as rebranding exercises, which try to convince customers that things have changed (when they haven't) or internal cost-cutting programmes. Often these exercises satisfy a short-term objective but prove costly and detrimental in the long term. Consider these examples:

Penny-wise and pound foolish

Recently, a global electronics manufacturer decided to reduce costs in factories that contain highly specialized production facilities. In this instance, the move was not to dig the business out of dire financial straits, but an attempt to meet shareholder expectation and maintain the share price. In this sector, skilled workers are a scarce resource, especially in some of the smaller countries where the production facilities were sited. To maximize cost savings, the company put together an equation that prioritized redundancies on the basis of length of service and age. Older, more experienced staff were encouraged to leave while younger, inexperienced workers were encouraged to stay. This approach cut costs but had long-term consequences.

Most of the jobs that the experienced workers had done were still necessary, but the less experienced employees could not do them. The result? Now this organization will need to look to an external service provider to supply these skills at a much higher cost. In some cases, the company may end up using the same individuals it made redundant. In the longer term, the costs to the company will be much greater – it is just that these costs will appear on a different column in the balance sheet, so results will look better in shareholder reports.

Shareholders may or may not be fooled. But customers and employees have become disenfranchised and disillusioned by these business behaviours. People increasingly realize that they cannot count on a company to consider their best interests, but must look after themselves.

Technology has changed the way customers buy

Whether for personal use or in business, people use the web to research purchases, investigating both consumer reports and other customer feedback before buying. So although most large corporations are still opaque and behave in an old-fashioned manner, exercising power and control where they can, the web enables many individuals to see through the smokescreen. This trend towards the 'informed consumer' is growing stronger as millennials increase in influence.

This generation has some unique characteristics. First and foremost, millennials are connected. This is the generation that grew up with social media, mobile technology and computers in schools. They are tech-savvy and know how to use technology to find answers and to connect with others. They are also team-oriented, preferring to work co-operatively with others, even when others might be halfway around the world.

Millennials have also grown up under the spectre of resource scarcity and climate change. They realize that unless something is done, they may experience ecological catastrophe within their own lifetimes. They also understand that humankind's well-being depends on its relationship with the natural world and other species.

Social and environmental focus is stronger and more global in this group of people, as is the desire for transparency in behaviours and actions. This perspective drives many of the career choices that the millennial generation makes. Finally, for them, work–life balance plays a big role in career choice. Work gets personal.

According to the 2016 Cone Communications Employee Engagement Study, two-thirds of US employees feel that their work and personal life are becoming increasingly blended and nearly all (93 per cent) want to work for a company that cares about them as individuals. The study reveals an increased expectation for companies to provide not only basic benefits but also an environment that allows employees to bring their passions for social and environmental issues to the workplace. Mature millennials (27–35) and young generation X (36–44) rose to the top in the survey as highly engaged employees in today's workforce. These segments are prioritizing involvement in social and environmental issues with much more enthusiasm than the average American. Two-thirds say they will not work for a company that does not have strong corporate social responsibility commitments (versus 51 per cent US average); and once hired, they are more likely to be loyal (83 per cent versus 70 per cent US average) when they feel they can make a positive impact on issues at work. Retention among this highly sought-after employee base is extremely important for businesses (Sustainable Brands, 2016).

Millennials want different things from their employers and from brands than the generations that preceded them. Most are very influenced by peer opinion and tend to be far less influenced than their parents by corporate advertising. They will buy from businesses they believe are authentic: in other words, businesses that honestly espouse and live their corporate values (which should match the values embraced by this generation). Corporate transparency, rather than opacity, and belief-driven organizations rank as 'highly important' for these buyers. Ethical trading and environmentally friendly processes and products are also a big attraction. With this generation, consumers are taking back their power in the purchasing equation.

How are most big corporations responding?

Most large businesses are organized around being in control – control of the business, their employees, suppliers, the customer and, if they could get away with it, the marketplace. To exercise this control with customers, companies must exert their influence early in the customer buying cycle before a buyer even understands exactly what he or she needs or wants. Traditionally, in the consumer marketplace, advertising played this role. But this 'consumer advertising' may be becoming an outdated tactic: today's millennials are not strongly influenced by advertising.

Savvy buying is also moving into the business-to-business (B2B) marketplace. Organizations such as the Corporate Executive Board and Forrester are looking at this area closely. Studies have shown that customers tend to be 60–80 per cent through a purchasing process before contacting a prospective supplier. This situation causes problems with traditional tactical marketing and sales practices because it is very difficult to shift a customer's mindset so late in the buying process. At this late stage, a business competes predominantly on price and service. In a survey, 74 per cent of business buyers said they conduct more than half of their research online before making an offline purchase (Wizdo, 2015). This buyer dynamic changes the role of B2B sales and marketing in a fundamental way.

What does this mean for traditional, large businesses?

Large businesses are losing much of the control and power that they once exerted. Of course, the huge monoliths still have money and power, but they are experiencing an increasing exodus of customers and harder, more cost-driven negotiations with other businesses. Falling sales, declining profits and loss of customer loyalty – however measured – are the leading symptoms of this downward spiral. As this loss of business occurs, senior management looks everywhere for someone to blame – suppliers, government legislation and departments in their own businesses. Typically, business leaders moan about their customers and blame their sales force. What they do not see is that their own structures, processes and behaviours are part of the problem.

In today's increasingly connected world, how can these companies attempt to improve customer engagement if they do not include the customer in their go-to-market solution? The customer is an integral part of the commercial ecosystem and businesses and organizations are living systems. According to Linda Booth Sweeney, 'In a spider's web, what happens on one part of the web affects every other part. The same is true of living systems, whether an ant colony, a forest, an organization, or a city. Like a spider's web, a living system is so intricately woven that no part exists in isolation' (Booth Sweeney, 2008).

Systems are the best way to envision a solution to the growing complexity in today's commercial environment. Adopting a systems approach means focusing on interrelationships, patterns and dynamics as well as specific components. The field of 'systems thinking' has evolved over the past 50 years and now offers a set of methods and tools to help focus on systems as the context for defining and solving complex problems, and for fostering more effective learning and design. Systems thinking helps businesses to shift from tactical activities and jumping from crisis to crisis, to move towards a less fragmented, more integrated way of doing things. The Value Proposition Builder™ tools and methodology enables businesses to undertake a systems approach. A complete shift may take years, but many benefits can be achieved far quicker. This book will discuss in later chapters how to achieve early benefits.

So, what kinds of businesses actually consider taking this systems approach? It takes a very brave company chief executive officer

(CEO) to tell shareholders that the business intends to take a long-term view that looks beyond the next quarter's earnings. That is why large corporations tend to look for quick fixes such as new sales training regimes, rebranding programmes and supplier renegotiations. In the long term, none of these approaches produce the desired joined-up impact.

What companies try

When a business does attempt to make a genuine change, how does it start? What is the first step?

Companies tend to start by focusing on things they can control, such as operational fixes that reduce cost and/or improve efficiency. Technical, scientific or engineering-run businesses usually take this approach first. Many of the companies that have used the Value Proposition Builder™ framework are technical companies. Most began their improvement process by investing in relevant technical aspects of their business. On the other hand, consumer businesses look to brand and repackage offerings, work that falls within their particular comfort zone. Only after all the technical and operational work was complete, or a new branding/packaging exercise implemented, did the executives take the next step and examine the strategic, go-to-market aspects of the company.

The businesses showcased in this book were doing well when they went down the path to obtain greater understanding of their customers and market. In fact, most of the businesses that embark on value proposition work are in good shape and want to improve their business. They all took the initiative to understand their customers *before* their companies were in any kind of trouble, trying to obtain a clear picture of what their customers valued as well as what annoyed them. By using a third party specializing in this research, each was able to obtain honest and enlightening insights. In all cases, the feedback shocked them. Up until that point, all the executives would have sworn they understood how they were valuable to their important customers. But their views were proven to be at worst wildly inaccurate or, at best, incomplete.

CASE STUDY

Glanbia Ingredients Ireland (GII) is part of Glanbia Group – a global nutrition company supplying ingredients and branded products into food and nutrition markets around the world. In the three-year period before engaging specialist support, GII had invested significantly in building a new infrastructure and streamlining the operations in all their plants. Once they had concluded their focus on operational improvements in their business, and had systems running well, they decided to examine what their customers valued about them, their business and offerings. Understanding their customers' views was a significant step to expanding Glanbia Ingredients Ireland's commercial ecosystem.

CASE STUDY

NATS is a leading global provider of air traffic control services. Headquartered in the UK, each year it handles around 2.4 million flights and 250 million passengers in UK airspace alone. In addition to providing services to 13 UK airports, and managing all upper airspace in the UK, it provides services around the world, spanning Europe, the Middle East, Asia and the North Atlantic. NATS's main focus is, of course, safety. Before embarking on a customer value proposition project, NATS worked tirelessly to maintain and enhance its unsurpassed air safety record, focusing on operational improvements and constant innovation. Finally, the business reached the point of needing to truly understand what its customers wanted and why, and what its customers valued over and above safety. NATS wanted to figure out how it could design an improved go-to-market approach that put customers, in fact all stakeholders, at the heart of its business.

Both Glanbia Ingredients Ireland and NATS (see the case study boxes), armed with information about what customers valued and did not value, were able to develop a plan to adjust their internal structures, processes and behaviours so as to capitalize on what customers truly valued, what innovations were needed and what things to fix so as not to lose business. Both businesses took a significant first step towards creating a new, holistic approach to their marketplaces and customers and were able to realize benefits very quickly from this joined-up approach.

Andy Head, Business Development Director at NATS, says: 'The Value Proposition Builder™ process gave us a new framework to engage with our customers and allowed us to develop the key design that underpinned all the organization changes we needed to become more customer-centric.'

What not to do

While it is vitally important to include customers in the change process, there is a very big step between knowing what customers value and then implementing an effective change and solution. Many businesses take the first step and use the Value Proposition Builder™ approach to obtain customer insights, and then do not take it further. Having listened to their customers, they go on to change only one or two things, and then carry on running their businesses as before. Gaining the customer insights is only the first step. The difficult part is changing the structures, processes and behaviours in a business so as to build on what customers value.

Below is a list of typical, tactical changes that businesses make in an attempt to implement their value propositions. Individually, none of these responses will make a significant impact:

- Do one or two things at a time without looking at the whole system.
- Reduce prices. When margins and/or revenues are threatened, some executives take the simplistic view that the only reason customers are not buying is price. Unless the business strategy is commodity pricing, price is rarely the key factor and, after a short-term flurry of buying, reducing price will ultimately reduce revenues and margins.
- Raise prices. Arbitrary price rises without good justification typically anger customers. After a temporary increase in sales revenues due to the price rise alone, customers start looking for other suppliers and revenues fall off.

- Rebrand product lines or the whole company. Today's customers are savvy. 'Papering over the cracks' or rebranding what is essentially an unchanged product or business will not fool them. Spending money on branding too soon, before implementing any genuine change in the business, is a waste of money.

- Create new products and/or services without involving the sales teams or selected customers in the process. Remember, products and services are 'for the customer' and it is always a good idea to understand exactly what is wanted and needed. Both the direct sales staff and the customer give invaluable insights into the best solutions.

In all instances, these businesses fail to develop a marketing strategy or fail to adjust the existing marketing strategy. Not only should a business examine its entire operation but it should also develop an appropriate marketing strategy to serve as a blueprint for all subsequent activities. The marketing strategy is a 'plan' that supports all 'go to market' activities. Without this, selling activity is not supported by the business and revenues do not meet expectation.

Typically, the sales force takes the brunt of the business focus where revenues and profits are concerned and management puts in place activities to 'stir up' sales efforts. Below are some common selling activities that don't work:

- Introduce a new sales training programme. Frequently, the reasons for falling revenues have more to do with the overall marketing strategy, business approach and aligned sales and company behaviours than a lack of selling skills. The most frequent problems affecting sales are conflicts relating to the sales process, the channels and how the business supports this process. One consumer electronics business spent £1.5 million on global sales training with zero impact before embarking on value proposition work. Focusing on selling skills alone can be an expensive mistake.

- Hire a 'big hitting' new sales director for his or her contacts book. The days of the hero salesperson who sweeps in and saves the day are over. Of course personal relationships help, but they only get a company through the door and speaking to the right person or people. Ultimate success will be down to a company's sales proposition. The business processes must support that sales proposition.

- Train technical people who work with the customer so they can play a sales role. This approach is common in highly technical businesses that employ specialists to do technical support at customer sites. There are many problems in trying to turn these individuals into salespeople. First, they don't want to sell; they are typically uncomfortable in the role. Second, their relationships are usually with the customer's technical or operational staff and not with procurement or senior management (the roles most frequently involved in significant purchases). Third, by making a technical support person the commercial interface, it undermines his or her former strong position as someone giving 'best technical advice'. The customer will now worry that the advice has some ulterior motive involved with selling.

- Fail to adjust sales rewards structures. In fact, failure to adjust the whole company's key performance indicators (KPIs) to reflect a new approach is more accurate. Rewards drive behaviours. No matter what a business says it wants, if the remuneration systems say something else then most employees, and especially salespeople, will work to the performance measures given. Most salespeople receive some of their salary or bonus based on these measures, so this behaviour is not surprising. A common situation occurs when businesses tell their salespeople to sell 'solutions' and then measure them on selling an individual component of the solution. It is typically easier to just sell the component. So if that is how the salesperson is measured, then that is what he or she will sell.

- Ask service-line sales staff to 'cross sell' and/or 'up sell' without giving them adequate training or incentives. This response happens so often in large corporates today that it is almost a definitive sign that the business needs realignment and a good hard look at its marketing strategy. One of two scenarios is typical. In the first, many different salespeople from the business each try to sell different things to the same customer (very common in siloed businesses). And in the second, a business acquires or develops new and different products and expects the salesperson to start selling them without adequate training or positioning.

- Fail to change sales material, specification sheets, price lists and other customer material. A new product/service or market positioning should be reflected in all support materials and in anything that the customer sees. Once again, using the example of moving to 'solution selling', if a company wants to sell solutions then it should describe solutions in all its literature and not the component parts. It should provide salespeople with solution pricing and not divulge the individual cost of components of the solution. Everything needs to be adjusted to support this shift in the sales approach.

- Fail to adjust all the internal metrics. In reality, a whole company is involved in the selling process. Everyone in a company needs to be armed with an appropriate understanding of both the organization's value proposition and its sales proposition. Everyone who interfaces with customers or potential customers – from the receptionist to delivery drivers, from warehouse supervisors to design engineers – needs to understand how and when to promote the company's offerings and behave accordingly. These people do not need to be salespeople, but they should understand their role in the overall selling process and be rewarded or recognized for appropriate behaviour.

As the list above shows, there are many false steps that can be taken in trying to implement a value proposition within a business. However, successful business change is possible. There are four key insights – based on leading more than 600 businesses through all or part of the Value Proposition Builder™ process – which, if followed, will help a business to move in the right direction:

1 Include both customers and customer-facing staff in the creation of marketing strategy and change initiatives.

2 Work on every aspect of the business at the same time, not just a single process or department.

3 Make strategic changes to structures, processes and behaviours before looking at tactical fixes such as creating a brand story.

4 Build on the foundation of good work already started or carried out previously.

Applying these lessons can have important positive impacts:

- Winning customers: everyone in the market (and sometimes within different parts of the same company) is vying for customer mind-share. Whoever gets there first with the strongest message, wins.

- Gaining market share: at the high-value end of the market, strategic companies will gain customer mindshare by selling at an appropriate level and delivering a single, appropriate message, while at the commodity end of the market competition will drive down prices and erode market value.

- Better margins: by approaching changes tactically and in a piece-meal, siloed fashion, companies end up commoditizing their own offerings and market position.

All of these insights lead to the 1st Law of Value Proposition Selling.

Law 1: the whole company plays a role in supporting the sales process.

To follow this law, a company needs to start with a holistic view of the business – and include key customers (and prospects) in this exercise. It then needs to develop and decide on its overall market approach and understand the impact this decision has on existing business structures, processes and behaviours. Only then should tactical activities that are in line with the strategic direction be implemented.

Is this approach complicated and expensive?

It need not be. The process does not have to be revolutionary, nor does it have to cost lots of money. In reality, tactical fixes often cost millions without producing results. The company mentioned earlier that spent £1.5 million on an ineffective sales training programme also invested more than £2 million on an advertising campaign. But what was it advertising? Nothing had changed substantially in the business. The advertising was papering over the cracks rather than fixing the fundamentals. And while the business did look at 'strategy', different departments used different consultants to work at inappropriate levels in the business, each with different briefs. This approach cost a lot of time and money, yet did not yield a cohesive strategy and did not include the customer. This is why it failed.

Why is including the customer so important?

An inclusive marketing strategy is vital for sales, marketing, product development and innovation throughout the entire business. One global financial services business illustrates how the organization itself can get in the way of finding the right messages. This organization had a 1,000-person internal research team that spent five years trying to understand why small retailers were not using its services and why their behaviours were often actively hostile. The problem? In its interaction with these retailers, the internal team looked only at the rational factors, such as price and the configuration of the service offering. The retailers, on the other hand, were acting on their emotions. They were angry with the financial services supplier and did not feel that their issues were 'heard'. This critical insight had been completely overlooked.

Buying is typically made up of two components: the rational and the emotional. In large businesses, there is a third: socio-political. By far the greatest component in decision making is emotional: after that, individuals 'rationalize' their decisions. So if a customer is unhappy with a supplier, then price and offering are far less important than making the customer happy again. In the case of this financial services company, its retailer customers were very unhappy with how they perceived they were being treated. This unhappiness led them to make business decisions that seemed irrational to the supplier. What was needed was a major behaviour change on the part of the company (and changes to some of the underlying business structures and processes) in order to placate customers. The in-house researchers had wasted five years by focusing only on the rational and asking the wrong questions.

Today, there is a high degree of dissatisfaction with large corporations among their customers. Most of these businesses have no idea how they are 'getting it wrong' from their customers' perspective. Either they don't know or they don't care. But they should. Very unhappy customers (or employees or suppliers) will go to great lengths to change their supplier, or even set up in competition to the offending companies. At best, as soon as there is a viable alternative, these people will leave – and that is the best-case scenario. The worst case is that these disenfranchised customers will be seen as an opportunity for competitors or new, disruptive businesses, who will use them to enter into the market. In both cases, the traditional large businesses lose.

Understanding different customer behaviours is also critical when moving into new and foreign markets. US businesses often make the mistake of believing that European customers – both consumers and businesses – think and behave as they do in the United States and that Europe is just a 51st state with a variety of accents. Nothing could be further from the truth, but many US companies take this approach. Europeans should not be smug: they make these mistakes too.

One European services business spent 1–2 per cent of its annual turnover in order to enter the Chinese marketplace. This company did all the usual rational investigations around market size and growth and, on this rational basis, invested in setting up a Chinese business. Then the executive team travelled to China to 'do business'. Intellectually they knew that China was a different country with a different culture, but in terms of business behaviours they acted as though they were selling in their own country. Understanding how your own behaviour differs from your counterpart's behaviour is vital. The senior management team did what they did in their native country. They wined and dined their senior counterparts in China, shook hands and left. And nothing happened. While this company did its quantitative research, it did not undertake qualitative market analysis or cultural research before making the investment. The result? It lost a lot of money and withdrew from China after spending millions trying and failing to enter the market.

Whether focusing on existing customers or new markets, the lesson is clear: include customers – both their rational and their emotional drivers – in any design or go-to-market activities. A lot of businesses are spending money on research, but usually it is the 'wrong' research, which doesn't provide the answers they need. Real insight and innovation comes from:

- understanding the customers' views and experiences – from rational, emotional and behavioural perspectives;

- determining what the customers value, as well as what annoys them;
- developing an overarching marketing strategy that incorporates this value as well as a realistic business aspiration;
- innovating products, services and solutions;
- redesigning business processes, structures, measures and behaviours to deliver value at every customer interaction.

Carried out properly and with integrity, these changes will deliver an authentic and valued experience for the customer.

To survive, companies must adapt. Everything needs adjusting around the customer:

- sales;
- marketing;
- customer service;
- talent management;
- and, above all, corporate behaviours.

So far, this book has looked at how today's customer has changed and how most companies respond to these changes inadequately or too late. It has highlighted how corporate behaviours have disenfranchised not only customers, but also suppliers and employees, all in the pursuit of profit and at the expense of people. But it is not all bad news. Overall the world is richer and people are still spending money – lots of money. So there is a big opportunity for customer-oriented, authentic businesses to grow and take market share at the expense of previous market leaders. This situation has also opened a path for disruptive businesses whose offerings satisfy customer need in a radical, new way.

What can a large, traditional business do?

Some companies have already started to include their customers and suppliers in their business ecosystem. Many have made early, tentative steps at developing their value proposition and then tried to implement the necessary changes in their businesses to exploit it. The rest of this book will cover the value proposition, sales and market positioning and include an examination of market strategy, customer service and talent management. Throughout, it will look at behaviours, structures and what needs changing.

In times of business crisis and falling revenue, sales leaders and sales teams get blamed for the falling sales. But, for most large businesses, it is not a sales problem: it is a company-wide issue and should be tackled accordingly. The whole company supports the value proposition and the process of becoming customer-centric, and it plays a role in supporting the sales process that flows from this 'customer-centric' approach.

References

Booth Sweeney, Linda (2008) *Sustainable Wisdom: Living stories about living systems*, SEED, USA

Kharas, Homi (2011) [accessed 7 June 2016] The Emerging Middle Class in Developing Countries © Brookings Institution [Online] http://siteresources.worldbank.org/EXTABCDE/Resources/7455676-1292528456380/7626791-1303141641402/7878676-1306699356046/Parallel-Sesssion-6-Homi-Kharas.pdf

Snyder, Tamara (2015) [accessed 15 November 2016] The 2015 State of Employee Engagement [Blog] Edelman, 28 August [Online] www.edelman.com

Sustainable Brands (2016) [accessed 28 July 2016] Half of Employees Won't Work for Companies that Don't Have Strong CSR Commitments [Online] http://www.sustainablebrands.com/news_and_views/organizational_change/sustainable_brands/half_employees_wont_work_companies_don%E2%80%99t_hav

Wizdo, Lori (2015) [accessed 7 June 2016] Myth Busting 101: Insights Into the B2B Buyer Journey, *Forrester Blogs*, 25 May [Online] http://blogs.forrester.com/lori_wizdo/15-05-25-myth_busting_101_insights_intothe_b2b_buyer_journey

Why businesses need a value proposition 02

The good news is that many of the businesses suffering from the symptoms discussed in Chapter 1 have made the changes necessary to adapt to the new market conditions. It is important to note that these changes really are possible. Not all companies are in distress. Those that are thriving have taken steps while business is good and invested in new strategies and approaches to their marketplace.

A road map for success

So what is it that these successful businesses are doing? How are they weathering the changing market? The answer is that they are engaging with their customers and studying customer behaviours, new buying patterns and trends, and then *adjusting their entire business accordingly*. The fast-food company McDonald's, following the resignation of its CEO in 2015, hired a new leader, Steve Easterbrook, who revealed his new strategy for the business. He is quoted as saying that he 'planned to strip away layers of management, focus more on listening to customers, and act faster to adapt to consumers' changing tastes' (Peterson, 2015). Winning businesses will adapt while those that do not will find their financial performance slowly declining.

For declining businesses, the first step is to acknowledge that there is a problem. Once this is acknowledged, the next step is to follow a more customer-centric road map to success. By shifting the focus to the customer, a company-wide value proposition provides the foundation for business resilience and growth. This approach follows the:

> 2nd Law of Value Proposition Selling: the customer is a part of the business system.

It all starts with the customer

Bringing the customer into a business's ecosystem is the critical first step. When businesses were smaller and less global, when there was less technology and people dealt directly with customers, this process was easier. Today, engaging with customers in a meaningful way is far more challenging. Specialist techniques, skills and a methodology are required to obtain genuine insights. But these insights are valuable – like gold – and fill a treasure chest for the participating company. These treasures provide the basis of the value proposition. As Ian Bolger, Joint Managing Director of Bolgers Engineering, says: 'Strengthening our value proposition was pivotal in the turnaround of our fortunes. Customer interviews provided us with extremely rich feedback and the interpretation of the findings also gave us a road map for future growth.' The immediate impact of this work was an increase in revenues of 25 per cent within the first six months.

So what is a company-wide value proposition? How does it differ from other options and how can it help a business adjust its structures, processes and behaviours to enable success?

Since *Creating and Delivering Your Value Proposition* in 2009 (Barnes, Blake and Pinder, 2009) explained what a value proposition can do, this term has captured the imagination of many. But it has also been misappropriated and misused. Various people have chosen to use the phrase 'value proposition' to mean a wide variety of different things; the most common misuse being to treat 'value proposition' as synonymous for 'sales proposition' or simply the 'packaged product'. So the next few paragraphs will clearly spell out what a value proposition is and what it enables a company to do.

First, the definition: a company's value proposition is:

Figure 2.1　The definition of a value proposition

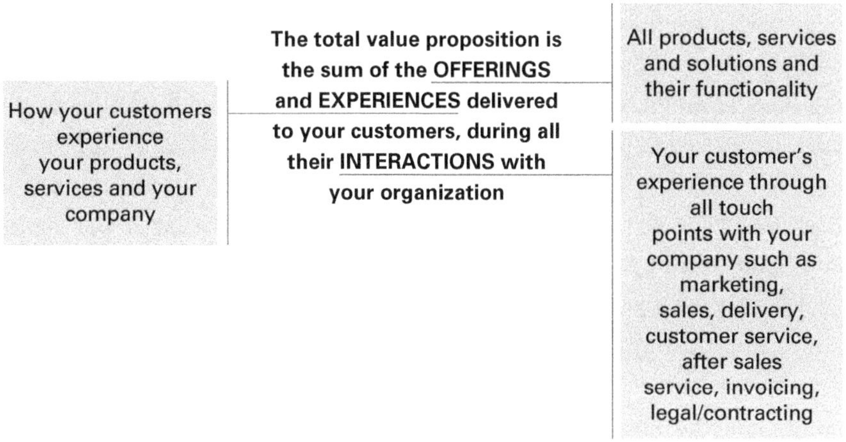

How your customers experience your products, services and your company	The total value proposition is the sum of the OFFERINGS and EXPERIENCES delivered to your customers, during all their INTERACTIONS with your organization	All products, services and solutions and their functionality
		Your customer's experience through all touch points with your company such as marketing, sales, delivery, customer service, after sales service, invoicing, legal/contracting

The value proposition is a blueprint for the whole organization, market entity or business unit, which enables the business to deliver genuine value to its customers. The value proposition helps a company to become more customer-centric. It is not a sales message, or a packaged offering, or a smart marketing story.

A company's value proposition provides the foundation for creating powerful sales propositions: sales stories and commercial offerings directed right at the heart of customer issues. In most instances, these will be aimed at individuals within the prospective customers who have issues to be resolved or needs to be met. Often, value proposition work will mean deploying a different sales approach as well as a new, underlying market strategy. Other business processes and behaviours will also need to be adjusted or transformed completely in order to support this new sales approach.

> 6th Law of Value Proposition Selling: ensure that all business processes support the market positioning.

How to achieve Law 6 will be outlined in greater detail in later chapters.

The wider business ecosystem

First, to understand how to sell to a customer in a way that harnesses the power of the whole company behind the sale, organizations need to broaden their view of the sales process.

The value proposition extends the boundaries for businesses so that the ecosystem includes customers, suppliers and the whole value chain as part of the business rather than being external to it. This approach enables even the largest of businesses to become customer-centric. It extends the customer analysis beyond interactions with sales and customer service to focus on the 'total customer experience journey'.

A customer experiences a supplier from every interaction – from purchasing through to delivery, payments and aftercare. So a road map for customer success depends on every single person in the business, not just the sales and marketing department. Mapping this journey from the customer perspective is key to understanding their entire experience journey (Figures 2.2 and 2.3). This company-wide perspective supports the first law of value proposition selling.

> 1st Law of Value Proposition Selling: the whole company plays a role in supporting the sales process.

Selling should be a team sport. Each business area and function has a role to play and all parts must be orchestrated towards a desired outcome. This approach does not mean that everyone goes out and sells directly to customers. But it does mean that each person knows what he or she can do to support and promote the company. Most importantly, everyone must believe in the company's value to customers and the problems they can solve. If this belief is not genuine, customers will sense the insincerity and begin to question the honesty of the business.

An example of lack of orchestration towards a desired outcome is that of the purchasing department of a large organization that had been targeted with bringing down the costs in all areas of the business. Reduced costs were that team's key metric. However, when members of a sales team urgently needed to fly to a potential customer on a long-haul flight, the purchasing team only allowed them to buy an

Note: In Figures 2.2 and 2.3, the customer experience journey is mapped out, including the order of key transitions, central questions and elements in this process. Having a clear understanding of these phases is crucial in producing a coherent path for the whole organization and its customers to traverse together. This understanding enables the various parts of the company to know and play their role in supporting the sales process.

Figure 2.2   Customer experience mapping – components and process

Journey mapping – the components and process

| | Visible to the customer   **+**   Invisible to the customer   → | Alignment of cause and effect |

1. Decide which 'lens' we are looking through
eg a segment/persona, an experience....
Customer Profile

2. Establish the journey stages
What are the high-level steps a customer goes through?
Journey Steps

3. Know their story
What is the customer's expectation, objective or trigger at each stage?
Customer Expectations

4. Establish the interactions by stage
What does the customer think, feel, do on their journey?
Emotional and Behavioural Reality

5. Map the touch points
Where do interactions happen and how do customers interact with the organization(s) along the journey?
Customer/ Organizational Touch Points

6. Map stakeholders
Who is involved in delivering the experience and what is it like for them (barriers, issues, strengths)?
Stakeholder Map, Profile and Journey

7. Map the delivery process
How does the journey get delivered behind the scenes eg systems, objects...
Organizational Journey

8. Define the pain points
Where is the experience breaking down for the customer and business?

9. Define the delight points
What works well for the customer or can be enhanced?

10. Define the opportunities
Where can strengths be leveraged?

→
VALIDATION, ACTION AND MEASUREMENT (Business Data, Customer Experience Measurement)

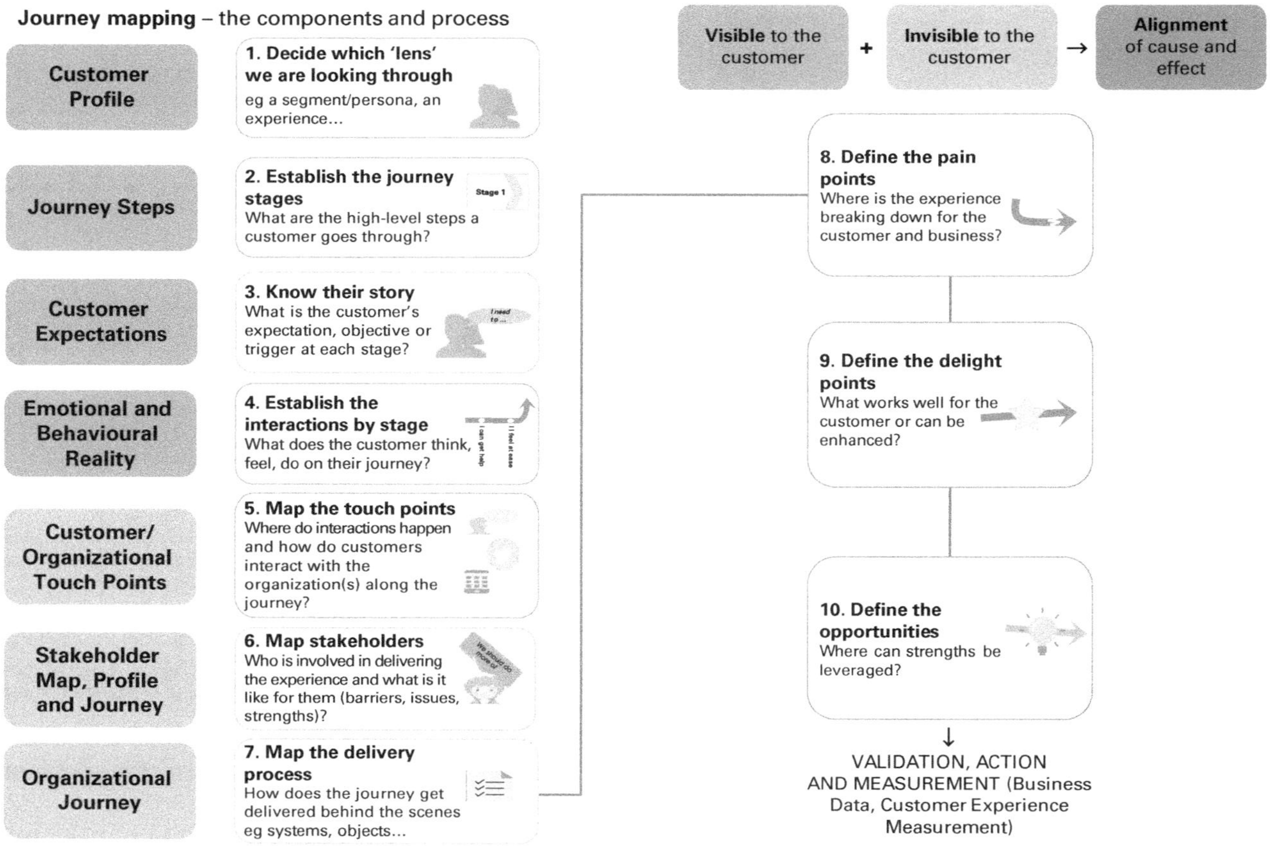

SOURCE © Customer Alignment Ltd, 2016

Figure 2.3 Customer experience journey

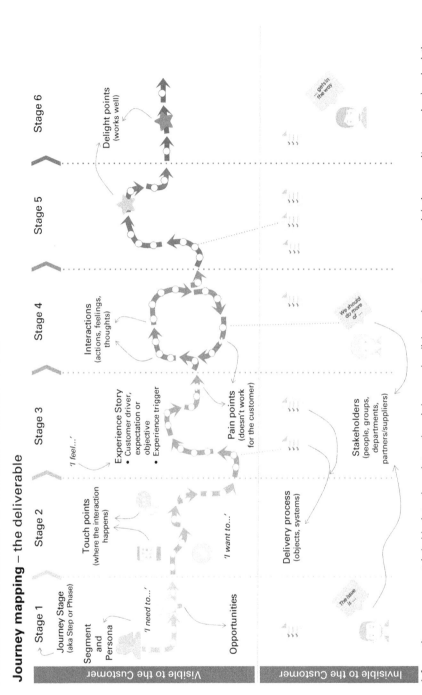

Journey mapping – the deliverable

Visible to the Customer

| | Stage 1 | Stage 2 | Stage 3 | Stage 4 | Stage 5 | Stage 6 |

Journey Stage (aka Step or Phase)

Segment and Persona

'I need to…' 'I want to…' 'I feel…'

Touch points (where the interaction happens)

Experience Story
- Customer driver, expectation or objective
- Experience trigger

Interactions (actions, feelings, thoughts)

Delight points (works well)

Opportunities

Pain points (doesn't work for the customer)

Invisible to the Customer

Delivery process (objects, systems)

Stakeholders (people, groups, departments, partners/suppliers)

The issue is …

We should do more of …

… gets in the way

Information sources: eg stakeholder interviews, internal workshops and walkthroughs, customer research (primary and/or secondary) and existing documentation. It will also include existing business data and any customer experience measurement, eg CSAT, NPS, Social Media feeds or scores (eg Trust Pilot or Feefo)

SOURCE © Customer Alignment Ltd, 2016

economy, multi-leg trip. The tired and irritable sales team were not in peak condition to negotiate effectively with the customer, who was eager to buy but drove a hard bargain. The sales team lost out and negotiated a very poor deal for the company. For a few thousand dollars more, the sales team would have arrived refreshed and in peak condition. If they'd been allowed to fly business class direct, they would have been able to negotiate a more profitable deal for the company. Every team within the company needs to be pointing in the same direction.

When properly directed and working together, teams can produce an impact greater than the sum of their individuals. Edwin Hutchins, in his book *Cognition in the Wild* (Hutchins, 1996), tells the story of the bridge crew of the aircraft carrier USS *Palau*. Together, the crew could dock this enormous ship but no single individual could describe how it was done. Many teams have this underrated and generally unrecognized group-based ability. Imagine the power of a company that can act with conviction, as a genuine team.

Pulling together

As a next step, a company needs to engage everyone – suppliers, customers and all employees – with clearly articulated market positioning. Behaviour change and communication is critical in order to gain traction with employees, customers and suppliers. When everyone understands the bottom-line objectives against which a business measures itself, then it is easier for everyone to pull together and work as a team to achieve those objectives – just as the bridge crew knew their objective was to successfully dock the aircraft carrier. When the objectives are customer-oriented then the whole business is on the right path to serving its customers.

Agreeing a market position, vision, values and setting objectives is, however, simply not enough. The business also must understand what needs to change so that everyone can 'walk the walk' and authentically bring this vision to life in the business, day in and day out.

For example, the top management of National Vehicle Distribution (NVD), the company we first met in Chapter 1, invested time and effort in repositioning the company in the marketplace and in the minds of its customers, away from Components positioning and towards a Co-created value positioning on the Value Pyramid™ (see Figure 3.3,

page 68). NVD also developed its new vision and, after much delib-
eration, came up with the phrase: 'We keep the world moving.' All
the management of this business now believe in this vision and have
undertaken a programme to design all the business processes and
structures to underpin it. Above all, NVD genuinely believes that
behaviours should reflect the company positioning, vision and culture
and it is seriously working on learning how to engender the right
behaviours in all parts of the organization, from the lorry drivers
who deliver the cars, to the customer service department.

Why start with a value proposition?

Why not just concentrate on developing new products to gain more
customers or to increase sales? After all, this response has worked
for some businesses in the past. Won't it still work? Recent market
surveys suggest not.

The Gallup report, A Guide to Customer-Centricity – Analytics and
Advice for B2B Leaders (Gallup, 2016), indicates that a company's products and services are not enough to gain customer commitment; they
merely give a business entry to the playing field. Customers are people,
and people are loyal to other people, not to things or systems. This
conclusion is not radical, but it is an indication of how far removed from
the human element many businesses have become. To gain customer
loyalty means ongoing engagement at a human-to-human level.

This research also indicates why a simple rebranding exercise,
however much money is spent, will not paper over the cracks. These
cracks are as much about the way a business operates, its systems and
employee behaviours, as they are about products, services or price. In
order to make an impact it takes more than just saying that a company
has changed – the company actually has to make significant changes
that are tangible at every customer interaction. If not, customers will
soon see through the marketing gloss and the company might, in
fact, be in a worse position, with its credibility and ethics under scru-
tiny. Many rebranding exercises are merely internally focused efforts
that make little attempt to understand the changes in the market or
customers. They attempt to mould customers' desires to the company's needs. This approach is the wrong way around.

So why engage with customers when developing a new market positioning strategy? The simple answer is: to understand what it is that customers value and will pay for. Also, engaging with customers will uncover what it is that will drive them to *stop buying* from a company and take their business elsewhere.

There are many benefits in understanding what customers value and then following up this effort by creating offerings, solutions and experiences that deliver this value and solve customer problems. Among these benefits are:

- Improved customer retention.

- Reduced cost of sales.

- Low-cost innovation.

- Higher margins.

- Greater spontaneous customer advocacy and – more importantly – customer engagement, an extremely important benefit in today's world of social media and the self-educated buyer. In the book *The Effortless Experience* (Dixon, Toman and DeLisi, 2013) co-author Matthew Dixon notes the importance of the low-effort service experience; creating a situation in which customers can solve their own problems quickly and easily. The book debunks the notion that striving for customer 'delight' should be a priority when looking to build customer advocacy and engagement. Customers prefer to solve problems themselves rather than talk to customer service representatives. The book points to research that suggests most of today's customer service interactions are four times more likely to lead to disloyalty than loyalty.

In fact, an authentic, customer-centric business can produce benefits to a much wider ecosystem, including happier employees, better-motivated suppliers and the support of the surrounding community. This belief is not new, just rare in today's business world. Béla Hatvany created two extremely successful businesses following these beliefs that grew from nothing to being valued at hundreds of millions of dollars, as described in *Putting the Soul Back into Business* (Howard, 2015) – Béla's story. He grew several companies over the decades, failed in growing others, but in each case learning how important it was to him to keep every member of his ecosystem involved in an ethical business. Béla pondered 'How do you measure the holistic performance of a company and serving its constituents in a balanced way?' Today he has a process. A third party, appointed by the company's board, conducts an annual audit to assess whether all the company's constituents are being well served. Separate specialists are hired to assess the different functions. Money remains important, and additionally, employees must enjoy working and doing their jobs. In Béla's case it took his determination and leadership to embed this approach into his companies. He summed up his belief by explaining that he believed that businesses should be 'for profit, for good'.

To take this point even further, Simon Robinson, co-author of *Holonomics* (Robinson and Moraes Robinson, 2014) says:

> The customer experience fully comes to presence in the experience of people who are not your customer, and the reason I say that is this is where we go back to values. When you don't really have these values you're only valuing people in terms of money and their ability to generate it for the company. It's really interesting; those companies that have genuine and authentic higher purposes don't differentiate between people who are their customer and who are not, because the authentic purpose is being fully expressed in every single behaviour; every part of speech. This is holonomic. You can't tell the difference.

In essence, successful businesses:

- know what it is that the customer loves and wants to buy from the company;
- implement a plan to build on these positive factors and attributes, including a new market position;
- create and document a vision that encapsulates their value;
- mobilize the rest of the company to help to deliver this vision so that the entire business is aligned;
- understand how to fully engage with target prospects and customers;
- supply happy customers who recommend and endorse the business, and continue to buy from it.

These companies also understand how to reconfigure their sales propositions and sales processes to support these efforts.

CASE STUDY LotusWorks

LotusWorks is a leading provider of technical services, including calibration, plant commissioning and decommissioning, operations and maintenance to the world's top manufacturers in the pharmaceutical, medical device, high technology, data centre and engineering sectors. Their customers include Google, Boston Scientific, Intel and Pfizer.

The challenge

LotusWorks had grown steadily but was beginning to suffer from commoditization and price-only-led negotiations with customers. They realized that they were operating at a commodity level in a crowded and competitive marketplace. They needed to understand what their customers truly valued about them as a business in order to enable them to successfully move from being perceived as a commodity supplier to a customer value-led supplier.

Tom Cafferkey, Chief Operations Officer (COO) of LotusWorks, attended a value proposition workshop utilizing the Value Proposition Builder™ process. Following this, he undertook detailed value proposition design work across the whole business.

Approach and solution

The Value Proposition Builder™ approach included interviewing LotusWorks customers, analysing the market, reviewing their existing service offerings and competitor differentiation mapping. This design work was followed by implementing the necessary changes throughout the entire business, which included new service offering development, sales bid management and commercial packaging and pricing, introduction of key account management, marketing and talent management.

Results and benefits

LotusWorks now clearly understands its value proposition and how to implement it through every aspect of the business, including how to communicate to customers via the website and sales bids and through account management. LotusWorks is now selling longer deals, with value pricing rather than cost-plus pricing and it has attracted some of the best blue-chip customers in each sector. Employee attraction and retention is the best it has ever been, with LotusWorks averaging eight new recruits per week. Within nine months of implementing the value proposition across the company, LotusWorks won six new large customers, with most of these being five-year deals:

> Understanding the lived experience of our customers through the customer research process made us drop everything we had been thinking about for the past 20 years and re-evaluate our position. It was that powerful. We changed everything. When the management team read the customer feedback, nobody had to be convinced that we needed to change. We introduced key account management, strategic marketing and market research, solutions development, value pricing and talent management. There were an awful lot of things interconnected, in fact everything was, we finally realized. When everything hung together it felt like 'the truth' and we all recognized when it was finished – the first design phase anyway. It doesn't matter where you look now, it all ties together. Our margins have increased and our employee retention is the highest it has ever been. Plus we are growing very fast.
>
> Tom Cafferkey, COO, LotusWorks

Awards and industry recognition since the value proposition work was completed:

- won a Great Place to Work® Ireland 2017 award;
- won 'Best for Commissioning and Calibration Engineering Services' – Construction and Engineering Awards 2016;
- listed in '1,000 companies to Inspire Europe' London Stock Exchange Group, April 2016;
- listed in Irish times 1,000 Top Companies list May 2016;
- LotusWorks is the Service Exporter of the Year – Irish Exporters Association 2015–16;
- 36th position in the Deloitte Technology Fast 50 Awards Programme 2015;
- winner, Irish Pharmaceutical Supplier of the Year Awards 2016.

The difference between price and value

It is important not to confuse 'value' with 'price'. Although price plays a role in value, the two are not the same thing. Value is what the customer gets from the tangible and intangible aspects of dealing with a company. Price is what a customer pays during a specific sales transaction. It may be a genuine good deal, a low price, or even a high price, yet a customer still may not value the interaction with the company that provided the product or service.

The National Health Service (NHS) in Britain today offers a good illustration. Although not a commercial organization, it offers services, and patients play the role of customer. To 'customers' or patients, the offerings are free at the point of delivery and yet often the way the service is delivered – long waiting times for operations and appointments with local doctors, the behaviours of some doctors' receptionists, the state of some of the waiting rooms – all combine to make patients (the customers) unhappy with aspects of the service. Money is being thrown at the various problems and, as in for-profit businesses, many tactical projects are attempted to try to improve the situation, but to date there has been little significant improvement. As in business, where customers can afford it they take their custom elsewhere and choose private medical care because of its customer focus, timeliness, choice and consistency.

Does the NHS provide good medical care? Of course it does, and at state-of-the-art levels in many cases, with dedicated and hard-working professionals. But does it provide it in a way that customers value? Much of the time it does not. And interestingly, much of the 'better value' health-care provision provided privately uses the same doctors and hospital facilities as the NHS, but their 'offering' gives customers a better value experience. Where money is not the main concern, value often comes down to how the customer is treated and whether the services are designed around the customer's convenience or that of the delivery organization. As with most issues related to customer-centricity, the key factor is about the perspective taken when designing and delivering the service.

In large organizations with high levels of customer dissatisfaction, employees also become unhappy and stressed. And, indeed, the NHS suffers from high stress levels and significant time off for stress-related illness among its staff: 'The NHS tops the league table for workplace stress' (Publicworld.org, 2013). When any organization – commercial or otherwise – fails to provide value to its customers, it will also suffer problems elsewhere.

How the value proposition approach can help public-sector organizations

Public-sector organizations have employed the Value Proposition Builder™ with positive effect.

CASE STUDY Enterprise Ireland

Enterprise Ireland helps companies to start, innovate and scale internationally. As one of the most prolific start-up investors in the world, Enterprise Ireland offers professional advice, skills development, funding, sectoral expertise and access to global networks.

In response to the 2008 financial crash, Enterprise Ireland redoubled its strategic focus on building sales and marketing capability in its client companies to strengthen their international growth potential. Futurecurve was engaged in 2009 to deliver a series of programmes in value proposition development to Enterprise Ireland client companies.

Having delivered to hundreds of companies over the past seven years, this programme has become integral to getting companies fit for exporting by working on their strategic value propositions. Exports of homegrown Irish companies have almost doubled in the past 10 years, exceeding €20 billion for the first time in 2015.

As Angela Byrne, Sales and Marketing Capability Lead at Enterprise Ireland, stated:

> Our organization has engaged extensively since 2009 in the delivery of best practice value proposition development for our client companies with our partners at Futurecurve. These programmes continue to add enormous value for management teams in bringing clarity to their propositions and strengthening their competitive positions for international growth.

As Karen Hernandez, Senior Executive, Client Management Development at Enterprise Ireland, stated:

> Over the past seven years Futurecurve have delivered their value proposition programme to hundreds of Enterprise Ireland client companies. The Futurecurve team bring a unique blend of theory, process and experience of practical application, which has supported our client companies successfully

to understand and build appropriate customer value propositions in order to drive business growth. Enterprise Ireland has recently engaged Futurecurve to support our client companies to innovate more successfully through helping them understand and ideate around customer needs and challenges.

CASE STUDY Aylesbury Vale District Council

Aylesbury Vale District Council (AVDC) is run by and for a democratically elected body whose purpose is to look after the social, economic and environmental interests of the people of Aylesbury Vale, Buckinghamshire.

Like many UK councils, AVDC receives less than 10 per cent of the council tax collected from residents and businesses. This money has never covered the full costs of the local services provided and central government grants have always made up the shortfall. Changes in central government policies have led to these grants being cut by 60 per cent over recent years, with the ultimate intention that no government support will be available by 2018–19. Since 2010 the reductions in government grants represent an £8 million shortfall in funding for AVDC.

Chief Executive Andrew Grant tells us how he and his operations team are developing a new, more commercial business model:

> We were just looking at the problem: we get £8 million council tax and it doesn't pay for more than one-third of what we do – to run the waste collection service is something like £4 million, so it doesn't take a rocket scientist to work out that very soon we could just be a waste collection service. This is a very important service for all of us but we as a council are so much more than a waste management company.

> We have made significant cost savings through our efficiency measures and making our assets work harder for us. We have saved around £14 million over six years but we now need to find additional, new income streams. In the business world a similar situation would be that if you only ever did what satisfied people 30 years ago, you probably wouldn't find many new customers. How many hardware stores do you still see on the high street, selling little packets of nails? There probably is a case for an independent somewhere but the rest of us go to B&Q or Homebase or buy online.

> Everywhere you look within our public services you see the mismatch between demand and funding. However more efficient we become, society

does not want to pay the levels of income tax that would cover the costs. We have to face the fact that society has shifted. We cannot go back to a golden age of local government. We have to change.

We've been very vocal about saying we need to be building a £100 million business in 10 years, which sounds a lot but only because 10 per cent of that, if we ever get to profit, is not that big a number and, quite ironically, £10 million on £100 million is in fact more than the council tax we are going to be left with in three to four years' time. We are saying, 'Let's be tax-free as well as grant-free by 2023', we want to demonstrate that we can run this business as a social enterprise based on the great things that we're doing, things that do not need tax at all, and that could be a new model for local government.

Challenge

We have a business that needs to monetize; I am trying to find ways of reinventing it so that it would be something that people would choose rather than just 'have to have'. We want to build choice, we want to make the case to customers to 'choose us' rather than 'require us', which is completely turning local government philosophy on its head.

When we engaged Futurecurve it was to try to give us some help with the concept of an overarching value proposition so that we could then organize our resources and our pricing around that rather than the old preordained value proposition for a council of 'You will have the bins service whether you like it or not.' We asked Futurecurve to talk to some of our council tax payers to see whether we could create a value proposition for local people that they would buy into emotionally and literally. Their work proved to be both critical and seminal in the proposition we are now actually presenting to people.

What Futurecurve told us is that 'You're trusted, you've got 75,000 customers who perhaps haven't known you for anything other than council services but are willing to consider what your value proposition is.' So it was trust, it was the 'why' of the organization that was important. That is what we will be putting back into our services so people feel that it is wholesome. We are connecting our residents to the services that they might want. We've now asked them what services they need and they are saying, 'We can't get cleaners, we can't get repair work done, we want to take the hassle out of getting home care, home maintenance, etc.' We've put on our website some ideas based on £200 to £400 monthly subscription for packages of care and repair, and overnight we have had 900 early registrations, residents who wanted to register for the service packages. It's not there yet but we've got the interest that gives us confidence to move forward.

People are saying to us, 'I'm not bothered that you're a council and you do the bins, you are trustworthy, I know that you won't get it wrong, you're not going anywhere.' This value proposition has been embedded through our early marketing activities and now we are trying to understand what the price points are and the potential volumes.

Futurecurve helped crystallize these ideas and the policy; the philosophy and communications with staff have flowed from that. Our councillor members are now using it, as it helps them to understand that we can turn ourselves into a business entity from within. A lot of people don't understand how we can do this: transitioning from one thing to the other without stopping the council and re-creating a company in the same building overnight. It's what I call Möbius strips, where you are on the inside of the loop and then you track the thing around and suddenly you are on the outside of it without having stopped and started again.

Action

We started this conversation about taking AVDC in a new direction well before we created our plans to change. You do not want to lose your customers but equally you need to transition them to what the business will need to be doing in the future. You need to have the value proposition discussion and ask: 'What is it in someone's life for which we are the solution?' You cannot sweat the stuff that the customer didn't want in the first place. Our positioning is that we need to be either helping someone to tick off the things on their to-do list, resolving someone's pain because they cannot get a plumber or enhancing someone's leisure or pastimes or social activities.

It is a failure of leadership if you don't reframe the world for people. It is not a case of saying, 'Join me on the barricades' and then saying 'Where did that Exocet come from?' because they will say, 'Well, weren't you paid a lot more money to see it coming?' To help with that reframe we have designed a commercial competency framework, identifying the behaviours we need, which is not just about selling, it is about knowing your customer, thinking from their perspective outwards, and we will be stepping everyone through a behavioural assessment this autumn that will lead to people being able to step into different roles, maybe from where they used to be to ones they would be better off doing. There is a sense of evolution and a bit of revolution in that we are going to be recruiting on attitudes, not aptitude, recalibrating the behaviours of our people with more of a commercial focus and philosophy and I think we are the only council that is doing this at the moment.

We now have business-to-consumer, business-to-business and council-to-council offers. We have launched a commercial arm, which has two brands: Limecart, which offers home and garden services, and Incgen, which has a range of business service packages. As we have been prospecting, talking to other councils, we are offering packages that help other councils based on our own experience of raising new income streams (such as setting up a lottery). Our lottery generated £60,000 for good causes in six months; we turned our £1.5 million loss-making planning department into a profit centre of £500,000. Only this week, we have sold two consultancy packages to two different councils. These are small steps into a 'peer to peer' approach to sharing our knowledge to get other councils to accelerate their change through the steps we have taken, sharing our learning rather than letting others go through the loop themselves. So those things are earning us money as well.

Results

Our value proposition is underpinned by the whole Digital Revolution and our deciding five years ago to be infrastructure-less in terms of IT. We are the first council to move all our IT systems to Amazon's web cloud. We want to reflect how people live their lives and a digital interface is critical. We launched 'My Account' this year, which now has 20,000 users who can now do online the standard stuff they need to do, like check their council tax or their licence progress, and they can now do this when they want to do it, when it is convenient to them. That infrastructure, software and staffing usually costs councils a lot of time and money. We are trying to do things that are common to customers, not just citizens; we use Salesforce, which is not a normal brand that a council uses. We are using cloud providers to improve our back office systems and have introduced cloud telephony through local providers wherever feasible.

It is starting to build from a zero base. In fact, we have been quite pleasantly shocked at how much has been achieved in a calendar year and how rapidly it is scaling, and the question we now have is how we resource the delivery of that for customers who are hungry for it.

Learnings

If you are thinking 'My business doesn't feel like it's working' or 'I'm stuck', then you have to be truthful about what you want to do versus what you are doing. Are you trying to spin off the business or inflate its value quickly, or trying to recover the customers you have lost to a competitor? Are you thinking legacy – do you want to hand on the business? What is the purpose of the business, what are you trying to do as a business? Being truthful will give you clarity over the purpose of your business, its purpose in the current context and in the future one.

Confront the brutal truth: what is the value proposition that is going to deepen your purpose or explore your purpose? And try thinking from the customer experience backwards – What is it that you are the solution to? What problem or pain can you solve? – rather than thinking: 'Why aren't they buying the gold teapots that I've spent 20 years making?'

Is your leadership up to accepting that this is a different business to the one you thought you were in and have you got the kind of temerity, the guts and the energy to switch it? Being clear about your business model also means understanding where the money will come from. What does the business need to be to fulfil people? By using the value proposition emotionally, technically and service-wise, it builds a sustainable and credible business that ultimately cements trust with your customers.

Realigning around a common vision

Creating a common vision about what an organization wants to accomplish is a good start: aligning all the processes, structures and behaviours towards achieving this vision can then follow. Most large organizations do not have an authentic vision beyond making money or reducing costs and have nothing around which to realign their activities. In addition, in very large corporations, making these changes takes time, and many face the pressures of quarterly reporting to shareholders. Yet some organizations have been brave and far-sighted enough to attempt these changes. They have found a way to design a programme that could be fully implemented in discrete parts of the business and yield measurable benefits in a relatively short time frame.

In the global telecommunications division of a major technology company, the business simply wanted to improve major global account management. Many companies in this position would have put all their account managers through a skills course, but this organization took a different approach. The management decided that they should develop a value proposition for (and with) each individual customer. In this case, the customers were extremely large corporations that spent significant amounts of money with this division.

The process of interviewing senior executives within the accounts revealed a great deal about how and where more value could be delivered. This effort was then brought to life during working sessions with each customer. As a consequence, the technology company realigned the type of work it delivered, how the offering was presented, packaged and sold, and how it solved the customers' problems. A senior vice president described the outcome as: 'an amazing difference to how we won better work from existing clients. I highly recommend using the value proposition building process to uncover where value is and is not being delivered.'

Both this technology company and AVDC consciously applied the 2nd Law of Value Proposition Selling – the customer is part of the business system – illustrating how implementing this law positively transforms business practice.

Changing perspective

After all, how can a business understand its value (and negative impacts) without asking the customer? It cannot. *Customers are the final arbiters of the value that any business delivers.* The challenge is how to extract this information from customers in order to obtain a clear and honest picture of what the customers genuinely like and dislike about doing business with a particular company.

Traditional interviewing techniques don't work. Surveys don't uncover the emotional drivers, nuances and the meaning of human behaviour. Directed questioning leads interviewees down a narrow pathway where much valuable information is lost. Furthermore, scripted questioning with 'deskilled' interviewers can result in missed opportunities to uncover rich and relevant feedback. A great deal of the most important feedback is not quantitative, rather, it is qualitative; it is about emotions and feelings and it is these that are crucial to the understanding of a customer's relationship and likely future behaviour with any business. The ability to view the customer *from that customer's own perspective* is critical.

CASE STUDY Global Financial Services Co

World-renowned 'Global Financial Services company' (GFS) had a long-standing problem with retail customers in Europe, whose reluctance to use their services was damaging sales and consumer loyalty. Psychology-based research revealed that the company's strategy was not connecting with the strong emotional motivations that drove these customers. Once GFS had used this insight to develop a new value proposition, it was able to devise a sales and marketing strategy that resonated with retailers, leading to an upturn in service acceptance and transactions.

Challenge

GFS had problems with retail customers across Europe. Around half were suppressing transactions – adding surcharges, refusing consumers, deactivating their accounts and avoiding becoming customers in the first place. Naturally, this was having a knock-on effect on the company's European business, hitting consumer loyalty and making it harder for the company to attract new customers.

For five years, GFS had tried different strategies to tackle this problem. Backed by annual quantitative research, it had tweaked pricing, offered incentives and run continuous new customer sign-up campaigns. However, none of these initiatives had any lasting impact on the retail customer problem. More recently, individual countries had developed new customer value propositions and sales propositions, with mixed success.

Solution

GFS now wanted to develop a Europe-wide value proposition to tackle the retail customer problem. Seeking to base this work on a deeper understanding of its retail customers, it chose to develop a value proposition based on qualitative research involving over 300 in-depth retailer interviews and retailer–customer observations, coupled with internal research.

The findings of this psychology-based exercise came as a surprise, revealing that the GFS customer strategy was out of step with what retail customers actually wanted. While the company was promoting rational benefits, their small retail customers were driven by emotional motivations, such as wanting control, gaining recognition and building trusted relationships. For GFS, this key insight unlocked by the qualitative research was a revelation.

As GFS had not understood this motivation, retail customer attitudes towards it ranged from ambivalent to actively hostile. Beyond the service 'brand halo', retail customers saw no value in the company's offering, especially as its pricing and service levels were not seen as competitive.

This research was used to devise a new European-wide value proposition based around the three value pillars: trust, choice and control, and the researchers then worked with the customer teams at GFS to turn these value pillars into a tangible strategy. This strategy included new products, a new service model, new working practices, and a new communications approach that started with a 'reparation' message.

Result

The value proposition project has been the turning point for GFS in its relationship with retail customers. Client, sales and customer service teams now all have a model that helps them to understand and predict retail customer behaviour.

Within the first six months, transactions from retail customers were significantly increased. A global advertising campaign, launched as part of this new 'relational' communications approach, saw 20 per cent more people using local retailers in 2014, spending £36 million more than in the previous year in the UK alone.

Customer interactions, the good and the bad

One good example of how *not* to interact with a customer is a recent interaction that one of our clients, Laura, had with a multinational telecommunications company. As one of a small handful of phone and broadband providers, it focused most of its efforts on technology and streamlining its systems to be cost-effective. As a result, unless a customer wanted to buy something, it was virtually impossible to speak to anyone in the UK who worked for the company.

At best, a customer could be directed to a call centre outside the country and speak to individuals who could rarely solve the problem and took unhappy customers through a closely scripted conversation. At worst, the only help was via scripted question and answer (Q&A) sessions on the internet. Customers who make the effort to phone a business are already frustrated: often angry and unhappy. Adding steps and effort to resolving problems only increases these negative feelings.

In keeping with this distancing from the customer, the telco was one of the first businesses in Europe to remove its executives' names from any easily accessible company materials. There was no approachable human face to contact. So the customer had to go through the company's systems to resolve any issues and these systems were set up for the convenience of the company rather than the customers. Over time, its customers became easy prey for new market entrants. So as other, easier options became available when new entrants moved into what was previously the telco's own space, the company was hit from all sides – provision of home phones, mobile phones and broadband services – by other entrants in the market.

Laura's story illustrates how badly the company understood the impact it was having on its customer base. Having been a customer for more than 25 years, she finally switched to a new home phone and broadband supplier. The minute the telco was informed that it was losing a client, it finally contacted her – a real person took the initiative and phoned from a local-based call centre.

The question was asked, 'Why are you leaving?' and Laura responded, 'I'm moving to a company where real, empowered people answer the phone. They listen to me and try to resolve my problems without my having to fill out forms and engage in web-based interrogations. Furthermore, they stay in touch and keep me informed of the progress of any issue. Can you do that?'

The call-centre person went back to the script and, instead of answering the question, replied: 'Because you have been such a long-term, loyal customer we are prepared to offer a contract at a reduced price.' Laura was outraged. The complaint had not been acknowledged and the response was even more annoying. She responded, 'Do you mean that as a loyal customer I have to threaten to leave you to be offered a better price? Why didn't you just offer me that price without my having to take this step?' The call-centre person had no response. 'Besides', continued Laura, 'I am not leaving because of price. I would even pay a little bit more just to have good service and speak to people who understand the context of my issues!'

This example is not exceptional. These conversations occur many times every day across a wide variety of business types. Laura was not listened to and could not speak to someone who was empowered to solve her problems. The result? The telco lost a customer it need not have lost. It usually takes far more motivation for a customer to change a supplier than just to tolerate an existing one. High customer churn and low customer loyalty should ring very loud alarm bells in any business. And the reason for churn is rarely just price; it is usually about company processes and behaviours.

Was the telco right or wrong? It really doesn't matter. In this case, what mattered was the customer experience. If Laura were the only customer who felt frustrated and angry, then the company was probably doing things well. If, however, many customers felt the same way, then they would be leaving as soon as they had a viable alternative. Ultimately, numbers provide the verdict.

Matt Dixon from the Corporate Executive Board, says of his research into his book *The Effortless Experience* (Dixon, Toman and DeLisi, 2013):

> What we found was that the majority of customer service interactions tend to create disloyalty. The reason they do, and I think we all know this as consumers, is that when we reach out to a company with a problem and we need the company's help fixing it to get it to work the way it's supposed to, is they force us to repeat ourselves and they transfer us all over the place to different departments, they send us to their website; we get turned round in circles, we can't find what we want and then we have to pick up the phone and call. Companies create disloyalty in these moments of need because they force the customer to put a lot of effort into getting their problems fixed. And so it's no real surprise at the end of these service interactions that customers leave actually more disloyal to companies. Customers don't want choice, they want guidance.

Not all customer stories are bad. Some companies do get it right and do the best thing for customers and for the business. The telco example (above) is the opposite of an effortless or 'frictionless experience'. An ideal frictionless customer experience is one in which the customers are not even aware that they are having an experience. They simply have their problems solved or their needs met. Companies such as PayPal have almost achieved this level of service with their customers and lead the way in designing processes that are effortless for customers.

Amazon is working continuously to improve its customer interactions. It takes a similar approach with some of its product delivery errors – even customer errors. Sometimes, if an item is accidentally misdelivered, or ordered twice, Amazon tells the customer to keep the second item for free. This approach is very sensible for a $10 book or other small item because the cost of processing the returns is much, much higher. The customer feels good, so Amazon's customer service ratings benefit. And it makes more sense to spend less and let the customer keep the item than to go through the hassle of returning it to stock. Virgin Atlantic is another company that did its homework and determined that sometimes, good customer service could also be justified by increased costs, with employees at all levels being given discretionary budgets to make unhappy customers feel better about the brand (Virgin Trains, 2015).

Virgin Atlantic and Amazon are both examples of turning a potentially negative situation into one where the customer feels 'special'. They also illustrate that focusing on the customer and empowering employees to make appropriate customer service decisions need not cost the business more money. Finally, they show that success is achievable.

Shifting to being a customer-centric organization can be done – and it has been done many times. However, the ultimate decision and ability to make these changes rests with senior executives. It is they who must decide to play an instrumental role in creating and living a company value proposition that reflects how the business behaves and is perceived. These executives must also want to create an organization that can deliver on an authentic proposition that is delivered in every customer journey.

In Chapter 3 we summarize how to create the value proposition that gives your organization its platform for change.

Self-test: is your organization product-centric or customer-centric?

From each pair of descriptive statements (**A** and **B**) note which statement more closely resembles your organization.

	A	Select A or B	B
1	Focus on the best product for the customer		Focus on the best solution for the customer
2	Your main offering is new products		Your main offerings are personalized packages of products, services, support and education
3	You create value through cutting-edge products		You create value through customizing for the best total solution for the customer
4	Your priority is on managing portfolios of products		Your priority is on managing portfolios of customers
5	Measures include: numbers of new products, percentage of revenue from products less than two years old, market share		Measures include: company share of most valuable customers, customer satisfaction, lifetime customer value, customer retention
6	Pricing is done by cost-plus or price to market		Pricing is value-based
7	Organizational structure is by product or manufacturing profit centres		Organizational structure is by customer segments, customer teams and customer profits and losses (P&Ls)
8	Your approach to your people is to give power to product developers		Your approach to your people is to give power to people with in-depth knowledge and understanding of customer's business

| 9 | Your thinking is divergent, 'How many possible uses of this product are there?' | Your thinking is convergent, 'What combination of solutions is best for this customer?' |
| 10 | Your behaviours focus on product experimentation and being open to new product ideas and innovations | Your behaviours focus on relationship management and searching for more customer needs to satisfy |

If you have scored:

- Mostly **A**s: you are a product-centric organization. You may want to consider starting a company value proposition initiative to help move you towards being more customer-centric.

- 50/50 **A** and **B**: your company has some insight into customers but is missing key elements by focusing on products. Working on your company value proposition will help you to become more customer-centric and make a material difference to your sales performance.

- Mostly **B**s: you are a customer-centric organization and you should already be reaping the rewards of customer intimacy.

SOURCE Based on an idea by Galbraith

References

Barnes, Cindy, Blake, Helen and Pinder, David (2009) *Creating and Delivering Your Value Proposition*, Kogan Page, London

Dixon, Matthew, Toman, Nick and DeLisi, Rick (2013) *The Effortless Experience*, Portfolio Penguin, New York

Galbraith, Jay (2014) *Designing Organizations: Strategy, structure and process at the business unit and enterprise levels*, Jossey-Bass, San Francisco

Gallup (2016) [accessed 24 August 2016] A Guide to Customer Centricity – Analytics and Advice for B2B Leaders [Online] http://www.gallup.com/services/187877/b2b-report-2016.aspx?ays=n

Howard, Tamara (2015) *Putting the Soul Back into Business*, Verve Business Books Ltd, Oxfordshire

Hutchins, Edwin (1996) *Cognition in the Wild*, MIT Press, USA

Peterson, Hayley (2015) [accessed 15 November 2016] McDonald's CEO Reveals his Massive Plan to Save the Business, *Business Insider* [Online] http://www.businessinsider.com/mcdonalds-ceo-reveals-turnaround-plan-2015-5

Publicworld.org (2013) [accessed 31 October 2016] The NHS Tops the League Table for Workplace Stress [Blog] [Online] http://publicworld.org/Blog/time_to_insist_nhs_employers_talk_about_staff_stress

Robinson, Simon and Moraes Robinson, Maria (2014) *Holonomics: Business where people and planet matter*, Floris Books, Edinburgh

Virgin Trains (2015) [accessed 31 October 2016] Passenger's Charter [Online] https://www.virgintrains.co.uk/~/media/vt/files/pdf/passengers-charter.ashx?la=en

How to develop 03 a value proposition

Now that we have explored why value propositions matter, let's explore how to develop one. To recap:

A value proposition is a blueprint for the whole organization that enables the business to deliver genuine value to its customers. It is the sum of all the offerings and experiences that you deliver to your customers, during all their interactions with your organization.

Once you have defined your organization's value proposition, you have the necessary foundation on which to build powerful sales propositions. The book *Creating and Delivering Your Value Proposition* (Barnes, Blake and Pinder, 2009), explains in detail the stages of the Value Proposition Builder™. In this chapter, we summarize those stages.

The Value Proposition Builder™

The Value Proposition Builder™ process follows six steps:

- Market: understanding the specific group of customers you want to target.
- Value experience: defining and understanding precisely what it is that your customers value.
- Offerings: mapping, defining, categorizing and managing the life cycle of your offerings around value.
- Value hierarchy: taking the external and internal views of your value experience and prioritizing them, including the cost component (price and customer risk).

Figure 3.1 The Value Proposition Builder™

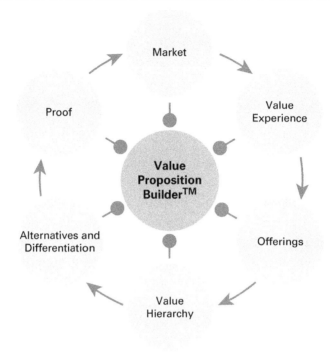

SOURCE Futurecurve, 2016

- Alternatives and differentiation: what the alternatives are to using your organization and how and why you are different (and better) than those alternatives.
- Proof: benefits realization techniques and evidence of your ability to deliver the customers' desired value experience.

Who does this work?

After 600 value proposition designs and implementations globally, based on the Value Proposition Builder™, it would seem that a multifunctional team from across the key areas of the business is the optimal answer. Usually the project lead is a senior strategic marketing person. A senior, board-level sponsor is also needed to keep the strategic direction on track and ensure that the board is kept onside and supportive throughout so that it will be receptive to the changes and innovation made necessary by this work. It is also important to take into consideration the various departments and areas of the business that are likely to be impacted. At a minimum the commercial departments need to be involved, including sales, marketing, product management and pricing.

Dave Brock, a leading sales expert and principal at Partners in Excellence, makes an important point about bringing product management into this mix:

> A lot of marketing organizations that I see today, even in very large companies, have a chief marketing officer (CMO), but they really focus on more tactical, outbound marketing. How do we create awareness, visibility, interest? They seem to miss the true strategic nature of marketing that did a lot of real market and customer analysis. What is happening? Who are our customers? What are the trends? What does this mean for our offerings? What is the opportunity? All that classic stuff. Very few marketing organizations today seem to own that and it has been moved to product marketing and product management. So it is important for the whole organization to be working strategically together as an integrated unit. It is important, too, that this is clearly understood and that product management is brought together with marketing and with sales.

It is therefore important to understand the differences between the various types of roles required in marketing and sales and how they integrate with all aspects of commercial function. Many organizations today are unaware of the specialized roles and activities required for truly customer-centric marketing and selling. This brings us to the next law:

5th Law of Value Proposition Selling: an organization must understand and be clear about the difference between marketing and selling.

The Value Proposition Builder™ is a structured, rigorous and proven process that starts from an understanding of your market and ends with developing proof that your value proposition works. Each step is valuable in its own right. And indeed organizations often have intelligence about one or more of the steps. But bringing them all together in a way that reflects back what customers want is the key to crafting a truly powerful value proposition.

1 Market

This first stage involves analysing target markets in detail, starting at the strategic, organization-wide level, then narrowing down the focus to sectors, regions, products or services, before looking at individual sales opportunities and marketing messages.

This exercise includes drilling down to specific organizations, buyers, influencers, original equipment manufacturers (OEMs), resellers and end customers. The analysis creates an understanding of the cultural and political nuances of the markets and the risks associated with buying from the company.

Key questions executives should ask:

- Where is your organization positioned in the marketplace? Is it where you want it to be? If not, where do you want it to be?
- Which markets or customer types offer the best opportunities for profitable growth? Who are the specific groups of customers you are targeting?
- What do customers need? What keeps them awake at night? What are their pain points? Are there discrete market segments?
- What risks do customers perceive when choosing your organization?
- What is going on in your target segments? What's hot? What's not?

What will the company be able to do differently at this stage?

Even after only one stage of the Value Proposition Builder™ process has been completed, an organization can achieve immediate benefits. It will be able to:

- plan sales and marketing by aligning with customers;
- enable its sales professionals to have significantly improved confidence and certainty about targeting;
- understand what drives customer behaviour;
- see how the company needs to adapt to meet customers' needs and to remain competitive – both now and in the future;
- understand competitive forces and identify the desired market position.

2 Value experience

Customer interviews

Fully nuanced customer insights are at the heart of this step and are probably the single biggest area of value in this process. However, obtaining these insights requires specialized skillsets and processes, because as celebrated advertising guru David Ogilvy pointed out: *'The trouble with (conventional) market research is that people don't think how they feel, they don't say what they think and they don't do what they say.'* Using a combination of qualitative, psychological and phenomenology-based techniques will unlock what people think, feel and do. It is vital that the interview is carried out by a trained, independent practitioner with experience of business and psychology-based research. Otherwise, customers may feel they are being manipulated through directed questioning to give answers the company wants to hear. At worst, some research feels like poorly disguised sales efforts.

The interviewer needs to uncover and understand the depths of the customer value experience from a rational, an emotional and a social perspective. Together, these three components enable the analyst to understand how customers experience value. It is also important to understand what customers don't value and to capture any constructive criticisms.

This approach is unusual. Yet it is fundamental to acquiring the necessary insights. As the artist Grayson Perry pointed out in an article in the *New Statesman* magazine: *'There is a habit of denying or suppressing emotions in business. This gives business the veneer of "professionalism". To be unaware of or unwilling to examine feelings means those feelings have free rein to influence behaviour unconsciously. Unchecked, they can motivate us covertly, unacknowledged, often wreaking havoc'* (Perry, 2014). So a business today ignores its customers' feelings at its own peril. Conversely, businesses that successfully navigate this process will reap unexpected benefits.

Internal company interviews

The external qualitative interviewer should also interview key company employees. This feedback will reveal what the company believes about its value to customers. In fact, carrying out this process regularly reveals a gap between what customers experience and what people in the company believe is actually delivered. At this stage, it doesn't matter who is right. What matters is the mismatch in perception.

Qualitative research allows a company to create a hypothesis about the issues uncovered and helps identify solutions. This hypothesis can then be tested with a larger sample, using a quantitative approach. This is where quantitative surveys can be useful for validating the discoveries provided by qualitative research; however it is essential to do the qualitative research first.

Getting inside customers' heads: a new approach to qualitative research

In Chapter 2 you will have read the story of the global financial services company that ran market research exercises over several years to try to understand customer loyalty problems, yet could not get to the heart of the issue. There was nothing wrong with the research itself: it analysed transactions and statistics effectively, creating a picture of what thousands of retail customers and consumers were doing. The problem was the type of research. Crunching the numbers is important, of course. But no amount of analytic power or big data can get inside customers' heads to find out their real motivations. And this approach is the problem with quantitative research when it is done in isolation: without really understanding what is behind a problem, you can end up asking the wrong questions. And if you do this, you will never get the right answer.

Qualitative research answers the 'why' questions

Qualitative research is by definition exploratory. It is used when we don't know what to expect, to help define the problem or develop an approach to resolving it. It is also used to go deeper into issues of interest and explore nuances related to the problem at hand. Common data collection methods used in qualitative research include in-depth interviews, uninterrupted observation and ethnographic participation/observation.

Quantitative research answers the 'what' questions

Quantitative research is conclusive in its purpose as it tries to quantify the problem and understand how prevalent it is by looking for results that can be projected to a larger population. Here we collect data through surveys (online, phone, paper), audits, points of purchase (purchase transactions) and click-streams.

Table 3.1 Where to use qualitative and quantitative research

Qualitative research – used to:	Quantitative research – used to:
• Uncover what is really happening with a particular issue	• Test specific hypotheses uncovered by qualitative research
• Explore the range of feelings and thoughts about that issue	• Search for and identify specific evidence for noted behaviours
• Look for patterns and perspectives between stakeholders	• Provide data on market sectors and subsegments (similarities and differences)
• Identify 'why': look for motivations, behaviours and other factors that influence why these stakeholders do what they do	• Identify and confirm data related to a specific and tightly focused issue
• Provide the basis for a traditional quantitative survey	• Look for consensus or disagreement on a topic
	• Determine the common characteristics of particular groups

SOURCE © Futurecurve

The limitations of traditional qualitative research

The solution is not simply to switch to traditional qualitative research – asking open questions and analysing the results. Here, the pitfall is that research subjects do not always tell you what they really think. Most importantly, they are not always open about their emotions, so they don't always tell you how they feel, either.

To get inside customers' heads and truly understand their motivations, a different approach is needed – one that uses social sciences research techniques rooted in psychology and anthropology.

Figure 3.2 shows the different types of research on a continuum. If you want to understand a customer's value experience in depth, it is best to start on the left-hand side, using social sciences techniques to 'see your business through your customers' eyes'. Interpretative phenomenological analysis (IPA) is one way to gain this perspective. It enables researchers to explore in detail how people make sense of their personal and social world. It focuses on the meanings that particular experiences, events, states or objects hold for individuals.

Figure 3.2 Research continuum

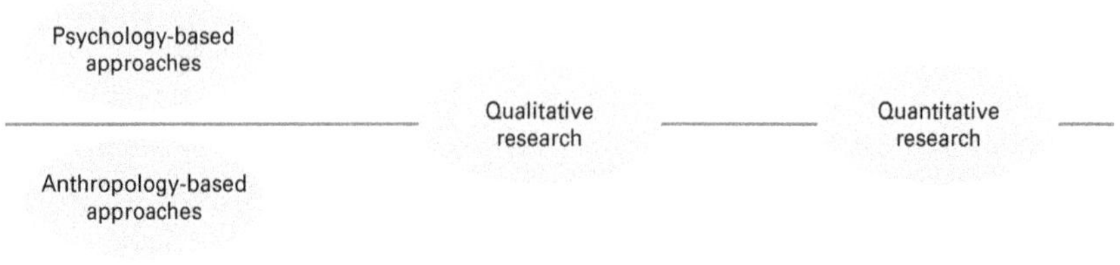

Psychology-based
approaches

Qualitative   Quantitative
research   research

Anthropology-based
approaches

It is concerned with the person's personal perception or account of an object or event.

In IPA, the researcher plays an active role in the research process as she immerses herself in the individual's world. She is concerned with trying to understand what the world looks like from someone else's point of view. The outcome of a study aims to 'give voice' to and 'make sense' of an individual or group's worldview.

When companies understand how their customers genuinely experience their company, products and services, this approach provides immensely powerful insights that can lead to transformative change.

What will the company be able to do differently by this stage?

From this second stage of the Value Proposition Builder™, the company gains a rich, deep understanding of its customers and what they actually value. With this insight, it can:

- create the core set of powerful messaging and stories for sales and marketing;
- improve key account management and go-to-market approaches for customers and distributors;
- identify how customer expectations are changing and what they are changing to, enabling the company to adjust its approach and offerings accordingly;
- have confidence in moving forward, with clarity and focus about its true value.

Note: Any negative experiences uncovered during the customer interviewing process will need to be fixed operationally.

> The big win for me was the customer value experience. The deep level of information and insights that were uncovered was astonishing. Not in a million years would my customers have shared that vital information with me.
>
> *Paul Foley, CEO, DreamTec Software*

As Matt Dixon of the Corporate Executive Board says:

> Two-thirds of what drives customer effort in a service setting is not what they had to do to get their problem fixed, but how they felt about what they had to do. And it turns out that companies can really think very differently and creatively in terms of creating a low-effort service experience by better understanding of the customer's emotional contact and trying to do things in the moment that manages that emotional contact. It turns out that an easy service experience is a lot cheaper for companies to deliver – it shows a much deeper empathy for the customer; what the customer really wants in their moment of need.

3 Offerings

The third stage of the Value Proposition Builder™ process is a detailed analysis of a business's offerings to customers, using a powerful tool – the Value Pyramid™ (Figure 3.3). This tool maps product and service offerings against the value they deliver to customers.

If customers have a clear idea of what they want to buy, then the inherent value of the company's offering is likely to be a 'component' or commodity. If customers have a clear idea of what they want to buy, then the inherent value of the company's offering is likely to be understood at the Components or commodity level of the Value Pyramid™ (see Figure 3.3, page 68). Customers that do not know what to buy may perceive the offering that can solve their problem at the Solutions or Co-created Value level.

The Value Pyramid™ places each of a company's offerings into one of these categories, enabling the business to manage, position and sell its offerings to maximum effect. It helps a business to:

- analyse the value that its offerings bring to its customers;
- map these offerings against the type of buyer and price accordingly;

Figure 3.3   The Value Pyramid™

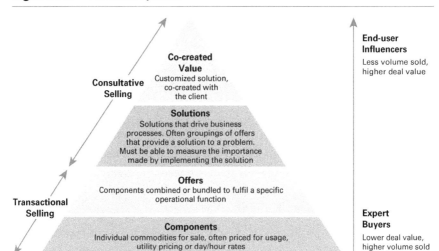

SOURCE Futurecurve, 2016

- ensure the go-to-market approach is right – consultative and relational or transactional;
- innovate, often at no additional cost, and discover underserved markets;
- create real differentiation.

Any organization will be able to map its offerings, customer buyers, competitors, pricing, margin, key accounts and even internal teams on to the Value Pyramid™ – and this process will reveal where best to deploy each to best advantage.

What will the company be able to do differently at this stage?

A business can map customers, competitors, buyers and internal teams on to the Value Pyramid™, creating a clear understanding of its current and desired future market positioning (Figure 3.4). This will:

- show the company's portfolio of offerings based on value to customers;
- provide a clear view about where offerings do/do not meet customer value-based expectations;
- enable the company to manage the cost of sale in bid situations;
- allow positioning for profitability and where to position for cash flow;

Figure 3.4 Worked example of Value Pyramid™

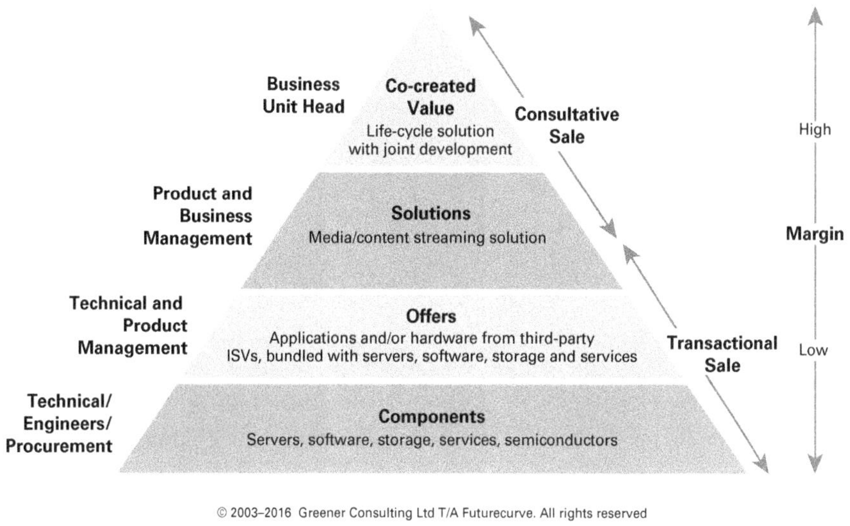
Business
Unit Head
Co-created
Value
Life-cycle solution
with joint development
Consultative
Sale
High
Product and
Business
Management
Solutions
Media/content streaming solution
Margin
Technical and
Product
Management
Offers
Applications and/or hardware from third-party
ISVs, bundled with servers, software, storage and services
Transactional
Sale
Low
Technical/
Engineers/
Procurement
Components
Servers, software, storage, services, semiconductors
© 2003–2016 Greener Consulting Ltd T/A Futurecurve. All rights reserved

SOURCE Futurecurve, 2016

- reveal where to position for best competitive advantage;
- enable low-cost innovation through repackaging and repositioning offerings;
- mean that pricing strategies can be aligned with customer value.

When offerings are positioned high up the Value Pyramid™, the person responsible for buying within the customer organization will change; for example from a procurement professional at the lower levels of the pyramid, to someone in the C-suite at the higher levels. So the sales approach will need to shift. We will discuss this shift in greater detail in later chapters. What is important to point out at this stage is 'The Solution Gap'. This gap demonstrates why, if you are starting at the bottom of the Value Pyramid™, companies find it challenging to cross The Solution Gap to move to a higher level (Figure 3.5). A firm that sells mobile phone accessories at motorway service stations, for example, would not be able to sell an enterprise-wide telecoms solution. However, a company at the top of the pyramid is likely to have the high levels of trust and credibility that would easily allow it to sell commodity products in addition to higher value products and services. Firms wanting to move up the pyramid from the bottom need a company-wide strategy: their salespeople or business units cannot do it alone.

Figure 3.5   The Value Pyramid™ showing 'The Solution Gap'

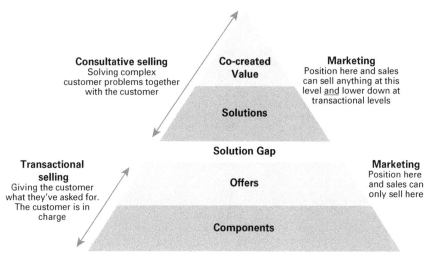

SOURCE Futurecurve, 2016

4 Value hierarchy

Value themes

By this point, a business will have deconstructed and clarified its value. The next step is to take the outputs from the first three stages of the Value Proposition Builder™ and use a value hierarchy mapping exercise to produce a refined view of how customers perceive this value. Then a business can begin the process of refining and prioritizing benefits that will allow it to develop a compelling value proposition.

Prioritizing value is critical. Businesses often get stuck at this stage because they want to include all of their key areas of value. However, only their customers will know what is of real value to them. Companies may have many areas of value they could legitimately claim but, crucially, the value experience interviews research will have identified the ones that really matter to customers.

Another reason for prioritizing value areas comes from behavioural economics, which shows us that too much choice slows purchasing decisions. Being clear, direct and succinct wins the day.

5 Alternatives and differentiation

Competitor and collaboration analysis

This stage compares your value against your competitors' value. Such an approach is a radical departure from most competitor research, which generally compares products and services – which is why it can only be done at this later stage in the process.

Useful questions to ask include:

- Which alternatives can deliver the best value to customers?
- In what time frame?
- Are competitors able to deliver this value cheaper, faster and better?
- What makes an organization different from and better than its competition?
- What does the overall competitive landscape look like?
- How do these offerings provide competitive advantage? And how can a business combine them to best effect to marginalize its competitors?

Other alternatives and substitutes are also compared, including the 'do nothing' and 'we'll do it ourselves' customer responses. Value propositions are compelling when they demonstrate why customers should choose you over other options.

6 Proof/evidence

The clinching element of a powerful value proposition is the proof that it works. The final stage is to design the evidence tools you need, such as case studies, testimonials, fact sheets and genuine total cost of ownership (TCO) and return on investment (ROI) models. Rational value needs to be validated by hard facts and numbers. Emotional value, on the other hand, needs to be supported by third-party validation, usually provided by existing customers who can talk with authenticity about how the company's value has impacted them.

Any proof needs to be backed up by clear examples, and show customers how this evidence is relevant to their business. This stage of creating a value proposition is also a very powerful derisking element for customers. It shows them why they should choose the

Figure 3.6 Value Proposition Blueprint™ with example outputs

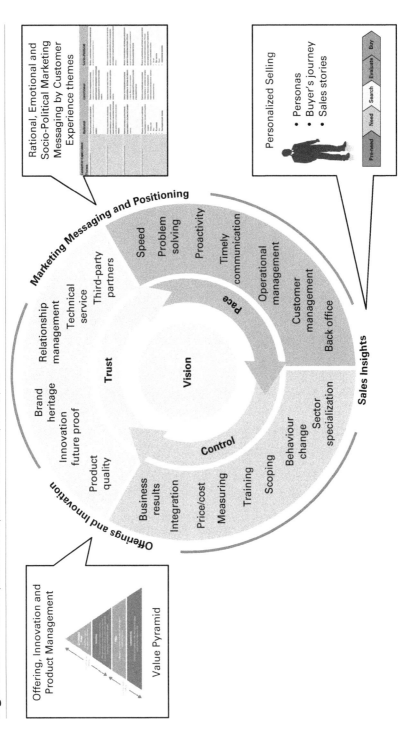

SOURCE Futurecurve, 2016

business over any other option, how they can build their internal business case and justify their investment, and, more importantly, the return on solving their problem. This last stage provides the foundation for creating powerful messaging and stories.

Value Proposition Blueprint™

A company following this process will now have a clear Value Proposition Blueprint™ (Figure 3.6). It may be helpful to think of all the detail that is part of this value proposition as being the company's 'treasure chest' into which all the company jewels have been carefully placed. From this central repository of value, messages and stories can be created for sales and marketing that have been carefully crafted and carefully targeted, and are truly authentic.

The Value Proposition Blueprint™ is not about fixing the sales team or the marketing approach. It is a systematic way of designing optimum customer experiences based on what customers and stakeholders actually value. It is a specific model for how to design optimal customer experiences for customers and the organization based on what customers value and what can be delivered now, as well as suggesting future innovations. Think of it as a design model. Wrapped around the blueprint is the overarching story of the organization addressed to key audiences. The stories are then tailored to specific sales propositions for specific customers. This final point will be covered in Chapter 6.

CASE STUDY

Mergermarket Group

Faced with a fast-changing market, business intelligence provider Mergermarket Group used the Value Proposition Builder™ to help one of its divisions understand and refine its value proposition.

The company

Mergermarket Group is a successful financial intelligence and analysis company that provides the advisory, corporate and financial communities with forward-looking intelligence, analysis and data, enabling them to keep up with the latest market developments.

A 500-strong team of journalists and analysts produces proprietary intelligence and in-depth analysis, enabling customers to spot new business opportunities fast and maintain a competitive edge. Customers who subscribe to the Mergermarket Group's range of products include: investment banks, law firms, hedge funds, private equity firms and major advisory firms, together with many corporate businesses.

The group has grown an enviable reputation in the fixed income investments market with products that provide in-depth and comprehensive content, which its competitors cannot match. Over the last 15 years the group has expanded, with over 1,000 staff in 65 locations across three world regions: the Americas, with the regional office in New York; Europe, with the regional office in London; and Asia Pacific, with the regional office in Hong Kong.

The market challenge

The Fixed Income Group, with its products including Debtwire, Xtract Research and Capital Profile, is a well-established and consistently successful part of the Mergermarket Group. However, the business is seeing increasing competitive threats in its major geographies and understands that action is required to maintain its leading market position.

Rapid growth has led to the development of a portfolio of products that are offered to customers as separate subscriptions. It is recognized that customers may now have differing expectations of their market intelligence providers and that current product offerings reflect the structure of the group organization rather than a customer's need for a solution, ie the customer is paying for separate subscriptions with overlapping content. The potential impact is a reduction in the cumulative value of the products and weakening customer loyalty.

Value proposition objectives

Mergermarket Group wanted to understand: what it is about its Fixed Income Group products and people that customers really value and how customers view the portfolio. They wanted to gain an appreciation of how to position these products in the financial intelligence and analysis market.

Research approach

The market environment was reviewed and 51 in-depth, hour-long customer and employee psychology-based interviews were conducted across three continents. The findings were analysed and a workshop was held in the USA where the key value themes were created for the Fixed Income Group products.

Findings

Without exception, the Fixed Income Group products were highly valued and respected by customers, who recognize their value and, in particular, the independence of the analysis and recommendations. Customers see the products as market leaders in their category.

Customers want the Fixed Income Group products to be successful and maintain their market position. However, packaging, pricing and lack of investment in the product database, for example into access via mobile technologies, means that the customers are exploring alternatives.

Mergermarket Group's people are liked and respected and customers want stronger and proactive business communication at all levels of seniority.

Three major value themes arose from the value proposition research: trust, tailored/flexible and timely. These themes formed the central pillars for messaging and product development, pricing and packaging. Each geographic area had a nuanced emphasis on the importance of these themes: for the US market it was 'timely'; for Europe, the Middle East and Africa (EMEA) markets it was 'tailored/flexible' and for Asia Pacific (APAC) markets it was 'trust'.

Working with the Value Proposition Builder™: a client perspective

Jonathan Reed, Global Managing Director, Fixed Income Group, comments:

> There were two things that really stood out. One was it reaffirmed a lot of the belief that we had internally and supported the changes that we were making. And I think it encouraged us to make further changes, and a really big eye-opening moment as well in many ways was that we were not 'solution selling' as much as we had hoped. We had aspirations to solution sell, and technology certainly was an impediment to that and that is one of the things that we were on the road to address but it kind of galvanized us to do that. That was a big stand-out moment – that we had to change the approach – and I think all of the feedback and messaging around how we could position ourselves, which the Value Proposition Builder™ framed, for us very much shared the direction we wanted to head in.

> We have Net Promoter Score, we have CRM and sales interfaced and certainly a lot of customer engagement in many parts of our business. Rather than trying to extract pieces of information from customers during meetings, which might also centre on something else, I think the independent aspect of the Value Proposition Builder™ process, the committed time frame with our customer, enabled the interviewers to really spend a lot of time probing and asking questions in a way that I think would be more challenging for us to do because inevitably customers would have other questions of us: about technology features, new content we are bringing online, commercial issues, etc, which can cloud the ability to extrapolate that information – so that aspect was really important.

> We had different representatives from different areas of the business come together for the Value Proposition Workshop and I think for the more

commercially-oriented team members who were present there were a lot of 'a-ha!' moments. For the non-commercial team it really put the business – as the customer experiences it – into context for them and perhaps helped frame, from a neutral standpoint, what our customers deem as 'our content' – be it our legal or editorial content or our analysis – and therefore they were able to take on that unbarred feedback and digest it in a neutral way.

Implementation programmes

The Value Pyramid™ really framed where we are and perhaps where we can go to. That was a centre point for discussion and it still helps us today to shape our decisions about how we move up that value chain. We can then focus on our ability to do that from a technology perspective, how to position ourselves, the messages that we need to be putting out to our customers, how we support the commercial process and bring our teams together to be able to speak with one voice. So there was a lot there, both from a content and a commercial standpoint, that we were able to rally around. It was also a very good neutral forum to do that with some unbiased feedback from the market – that was very successful for us.

I went region by region in January and February this year, taking a lot of the discussion points and actually sitting down with the team and talking with them about why we needed to change our approach, what our customers were saying and sharing some of that feedback with each region. And then starting to use those forums to get input from those commercial teams as to what they thought that change should be and really enable us to get buy-in from them, to check how to position ourselves to really serve our customers in the best possible way. And so it was a good jumping-off point, again with an independent viewpoint – sharing the views of customers helped really reinforce the need to position ourselves differently and change the commercial structure and set-up. We were then able to implement quite a lot of change in each of the regions, which we felt needed to happen but it was a very important catalyst to rally people around – and as I have said, an independent view of what our customers are saying and how we could serve them better. So I think there was a lot more done around the commercial change aspect of how we were set up – and understanding that we were making the technology changes to support that.

At the end of the process we had the master global overview, which took components from each region, and I think one of the real benefits was boiling it down to messages that were transferable across geographic regions. Within each region with its own idiosyncrasies we framed our market positioning and issues, which were perhaps more of a concern in one region over another but we came away with a consistent set for the three regional teams, which I still talk about today – a consistent set of positioning messages that we use to centre on with each region's own adjustments. So it was a very, very helpful format by which to showcase the overarching message and support the areas we need to focus on and the changes we are making.

CASE STUDY

GlycoSelect

Start-up GlycoSelect used the value proposition process to shift its focus away from its technology and towards customer needs.

Based on investment funding, GlycoSelect is a start-up with less than €1 million revenue and 10 employees. It was born of an industry-academia collaboration to address problems associated with the development, analysis and production of biopharmaceutical products. The resultant technology uses an innovative separation method that enables improved product analysis and more effective manufacturing processes.

GlycoSelect is currently targeting the product purification segment within the pharmaceutical market, where 95 per cent of all new drugs are biopharmaceuticals.

CEO Robert Dunne comments:

We are involved in a very specific area of science: glycobiology. It is becoming increasingly important but it is a relatively young part of biology. It has grown in the last 20 to 30 years and we are now coming to the point where people understand that it is very important in physiology: for example, many new pharmaceuticals are based on the science that our technology works on.

Challenge

We have very little in terms of sales and any sales increase we have will be down to product licensing deals, so our sales are very granular. The pharmaceutical industry is notoriously conservative. We may have our first technology licence this year and it is two years since the potential customer called us to discuss the licence.

Solution

When you are scientists and selling to scientists, you may think you know your customer. But in reality that may not be the 'real customer' because the lab scientist is generally not the person who signs the cheques.

It is a complex market, and being able to understand that, put it in basic terms and to be able to refocus our sales pitch and customer experience is important for our company's future. This is the area where we are focusing on now: understanding our customer experience. I think scientists have a problem – because they are handling the same thing, they think they know what the other guy wants and in fact they don't. I'll give you a very good example. One of our development advisors uses the same equipment that we put our technology on to. Despite the fact that he uses the same piece of kit applied to plastics, he does not understand our technology as it is applied to pharmaceuticals. So two scientists can use the same equipment but they still have to have the technology explained to them. For that reason, we have taken the decision that we will always have a scientist at every customer meeting unless there is a really good reason why they should not be there.

We identified that having closer engagement with our customers by making our scientists available to them, to advise them and visit more, was a customer need we were fulfilling, but not fully recognizing the significant value it had for customers. By increasing these interactions we have increased sales, especially repeat ones, but also gained new insights into other applications for our technology. We were already providing added value but had not recognized its importance to our customers. We have definitely changed our priorities when dealing with customers.

Result

Principally the Value Proposition Builder™ process gave us focus, I think that has been the main advantage that I've gained from it. Our technology is quite complicated and one can get very parochial about it – taking my focus away from the technology has given me the ability to go back to the business and say okay, well what is the value proposition that we are giving to our customers? That has been great and in fact we are working on that now and, for example, we put our scientists in front of customers more. We have made adjustments in two ways: putting the focus on to the business and actually implementing the reality of what I learnt.

We also identified our branding as being very weak, in fact we don't do any, and I'm working on that at the moment. I've found a mentor from Enterprise Ireland who will help me with the branding work, and that should be in place by year end. The reason for stronger branding is because we could get swamped by our customers' brands as they all happen to be larger companies that use our technology on their equipment. We need an 'Intel Inside' strategy.

Learning

It has given us a structure, the Value Proposition Builder™ has become our template. One can do business canvasses and all the rest but this is a bit more powerful because it directs the strategy, the positioning and it has enabled us to focus on the customers a lot more.

Future

Our value proposition is now based on following this analysis – we know we improve manufacturing and improve product analysis in the pharmaceutical industry. And that's it, that's the value proposition, and we reinforce that with our expert advice. This is a far easier sell to investors, so I think what I'm saying is that, having gone through the process with Futurecurve, I started on the value proposition journey not really believing it was going to change anything, but I now know what my business is really about – as distinct from what the science is really about.

For further case studies of companies that have been through the Value Proposition Builder™ process, see Appendix 2.

See things from the customer's viewpoint

The value experience step in the Value Proposition Builder™ process highlights that one of the most critical areas is in understanding issues and needs from the customer's perspective. It is all about perspective. In particular, learning how to see things the way the customer sees them. Many businesses, especially those that are technically focused, find this shift particularly difficult. They struggle to make the leap from thinking about their own capabilities and products to thinking about what the customer really wants, from his or her own point of view.

Changing your frame of reference to see things from your customer's perspective is, in essence, like practising empathy on a corporate scale.

How do you 'reframe'? The following exercises are tried-and-tested ways to shift your perspective. Do try them for yourself:

1 Walk with an expert: in Alexandra Horowitz's book *On Looking*, she walks around familiar places with various experts on typography, public spaces or geology in order to gain a new perspective. This approach mirrors using consultants who will bring in people from diverse backgrounds with different experiences and expertise.

2 Change your physical position: if you are a factory boss and you always enter the factory by the same door each day, always take the same route to your office, always have lunch in the same place, then deliberately try changing this routine. Do things differently. Mix it up. See if you start to notice different things about your regular day.

3 Zoom in and zoom out: imagine that you are looking through a viewfinder on a camera and you are zooming in on something nearby. Take a few moments to focus and see the detail and richness in that thing. Then imagine you are zooming out and looking at that same thing but now you are seeing it in the context of its relationships with everything else around it.

References

Barnes, Cindy, Blake, Helen and Pinder, David (2009) *Creating and Delivering Your Value Proposition*, Kogan Page, London

Perry, Grayson (2014) [accessed 24 August 2016] Grayson Perry: The Rise and Fall of Default Man, *New Statesman* [Online] http://www.newstatesman.com/culture/2014/10/grayson-perry-rise-and-fall-default-man

How to translate a value proposition into a sales proposition

Every day when your salespeople meet customers and prospects they are out there creating sales propositions. But are they selling what is best for your business goals? Are they selling what the customer really needs or wants? These are important questions, because if your sales activity is out of sync with your overarching value proposition, it could at best be wasted effort and, at worst, counterproductive.

It is not uncommon for businesses to put time and effort into developing and refining a value proposition, and then to miss out the crucial next step of translating it into how they go to market. For example, if a business has decided that it is now a solutions business, but salespeople are still pushing product and focusing on price, a new value proposition will not deliver the desired results. Your customers will not take you seriously if you try to introduce a new value proposition without planning it carefully first. Imagine if value retailers like Wal-Mart or Primark started selling Tiffany jewellery. Their customers would not be in the market for these expensive items and Tiffany customers would not go looking for them in low-cost retailers. Commodity businesses trying to make the shift to solution selling are exposed to precisely the same credibility or value gap.

It is also crucial to get the pitch right for different customers. For example, if a company sells to both business-to-business (B2B) and business-to-consumer (B2C) markets, the concept of 'confidence' in its value proposition would need to be articulated differently for each audience. Business customers might be focused on how this could affect their standing among their peers ('no one ever got fired for buying IBM'), while a consumer's main concern might be around the feeling that a device will not fail. Looking at the same example through the lens of different job specialisms, finance directors might see 'confidence' as something that helps with cost control; while IT specialists could be mostly thinking about reliability and uptime. Each function will have a 'job to be done', an idea created by Professor Clayton Christensen and Michael Raynor in their book *The Innovator's Solution* (Christensen and Raynor, 2003). On Christensen's website (Christensen Institute, 2016) he points out:

> The jobs-to-be-done framework emerged as a helpful way to look at customer motivations in business settings. Conventional marketing techniques teach us to frame customers by attributes – using age ranges, race, marital status, and other categories that ultimately create products and entire categories too focused on what companies want to sell, rather than on what customers actually need. The jobs-to-be-done framework is a tool for evaluating the circumstances that arise in customers' lives. Customers rarely make buying decisions around what the 'average' customer in their category may do – but they often buy things because they find themselves with a problem they would like to solve. With an understanding of the 'job' for which customers find themselves 'hiring' a product or service, companies can more accurately develop and market products well-tailored to what customers are already trying to do.

So new sales propositions need to be carefully planned and framed appropriately for different markets and audiences. How do you do this?

There are several steps to the process, the first two of which are taken care of in the Value Proposition Builder™ process:

1 Understand what customers value.

2 Understand how they see you – in relation to your value.

3 Identify your core skills and capabilities.

4 Decide where to place sales propositions on the Value Pyramid™.

5 Create customer-centric sales propositions.

6 Choose the right sales approach.

7 Frame the sales propositions with the right story.

8 Make sure that everything you do supports this sales approach.

By the time a business has designed a new value proposition (see Chapter 3) it will know the answers to the first two steps: what customers value and how they perceive the business. Let's recap these and then explore all the steps needed to turn a value proposition into a sales proposition. We will also look at case studies of two companies that have successfully achieved this.

Understanding what customers value

The outcome of good value proposition design work is a finely crafted set of organizational attributes. These are the 'company treasures' – the unique characteristics that are known and valued by customers and that give a business its unique characteristic. They can be summarized at a high level and used to focus all subsequent activities.

For example, in one company the attributes might be:

- expert;
- trusted;
- innovative.

For another, they could be:

- reliable;
- safe;
- responsive.

The themes above look deceptively simple, so for the full detail please review the section in Chapter 3 on the Value Proposition Blueprint™. Typically, value proposition work uncovers three to five key attributes that are the top reasons for customers to do business with a particular company. Any credible sales proposition should use and build on them.

How customers see you

How are you viewed? As a Components supplier or a Solutions company? Customer interviews in the value proposition design stage will have revealed what customers think of you. If you have not carried out that stage, this quick diagnostic will give you a 'read' on how customers see you.

Does the customer always provide a 'request for proposal' (RFP) or 'request for information' (RFI)? If yes, then your business is probably being seen at the 'Components' or 'Offers' level. (see Figure 4.1).

Of course, some markets (for example public-sector organizations) must always issue a formal bidding document. However, when a RFP appears out of the blue and it is the first time that a business has heard of the opportunity, there may well be another company already involved with the customer who is better positioned. When a business has not been consulted about how to structure a solution, the customer believes it knows what it needs. It will have obtained this view from someone (often a competitor) – and will buy accordingly.

With whom do sales discussions take place?

Figure 4.1   The Value Pyramid™

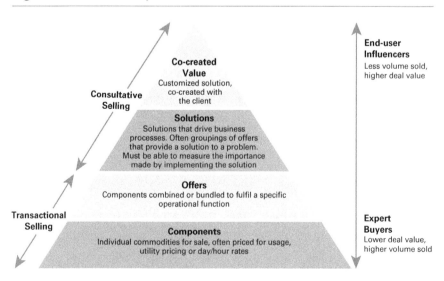

© 2003–2016 Greener Consulting Ltd T/A Futurecurve. All rights reserved

SOURCE Futurecurve, 2016

If your dealings are mostly with procurement or purchasing specialists, then you are being seen as a supplier at the Components or Offers level. Any time a salesperson cannot speak to the individual within an organization who owns the need, the chances are that the sale will be transactional and at the Components level of the Value Pyramid™. On the other hand, if most dealings are with the people who own the business problem to be resolved, then it is possible that the customer will be open to a more consultative style. Unless you have access to the individual(s) within the prospective customer who owns the need being solved, it is virtually impossible to sell consultatively.

Has an RFI or RFP come out of the blue from a company who has never purchased anything from your business?

In general, by the time any RFI/RFP is produced, the customer already believes they understand what needs to be purchased. The opportunity to sell consultatively and offer 'a solution' has passed unless your salespeople have the skills to push back hard and redefine the solution. Most procurement departments like to set up competitive bidding, even if there is already a favoured supplier. So they send out requests for proposals to many other companies to get negotiating leverage with the preferred supplier. Unless a salesperson can gain access to the individual with the business need (not the procurement department) and change the specifications, the chances of winning this sort of opportunity are almost zero.

Identify your core skills and capabilities

The next step is to assess honestly and list the business's core skills and capabilities. In an information services business, these might include communication skills, data sources and/or analytical skills. For a manufacturing company making high-function components, the core skills and assets could be manufacturing plant, R&D capability, supply chain management and specialist manufacturing skills.

The point of this exercise is to understand the building blocks with which you assemble a sales proposition. There is nothing to stop the information services company in the previous paragraph from selling its raw data – but there is much greater value in selling an analytical newsletter or update. Similarly, the manufacturing business could sell its R&D services as a separate entity, or subcontract portions of its plant to other manufacturers, but then it would be in a different business from making components. Selling individual core capabilities creates businesses that are positioned differently. By combining these building blocks into sales propositions, the company can reposition its capabilities higher up the Value Pyramid™. In neither example has the business created a new capability – it has merely reconfigured the pieces to present them to the marketplace in a different way.

This reconfiguring is also a highly effective way to achieve low-cost, high-impact innovation, as long as sales teams have the right skills and behaviours to sell this new proposition. As a reminder, take a look at the Value Pyramid™ section in Chapter 3.

Decide where to place propositions on the Value Pyramid™

Sometimes, when businesses undertake value proposition work, they are shocked to find that while they think they provide high-value services, their customers see them as 'commodity' suppliers. This view is often out of step with how the business sees itself. How did this happen? Typically this happens when a business uses an inappropriate sales approach (often transactional and focused on competitive pricing). When, in response to customer demand for lower prices, a business always reduces its prices, the business has in effect 'commoditized' itself!

There is nothing wrong with commodity positioning as long as it is part of a well-thought-out business strategy. Some companies may wish to position themselves on the component level and that might well be the best strategy for them. However, many businesses invest time and money in capabilities that could enable them to position their businesses higher up, and so gain greater revenue from their sales. It is these businesses that should consider exploring a new way of presenting their offerings.

How can a business determine where to position itself on the Value Pyramid™?

There are no hard and fast rules. However, Solutions businesses share some common characteristics:

- market leadership in terms of R&D;
- market leadership in terms of dominant market position;
- unique products or services;
- sole vendor in a particular niche or geography.

Any or all of these attributes put the selling business in a position of control – either through knowledge (product innovation or service expertise) or market dominance. Any business that possesses three out of four of these attributes, and still deploys transactional selling, is leaving money on the table and weakening its own market positioning. However, a company that possesses none of them can still try to position itself as a Solutions supplier, although it will be a little more challenging. In these circumstances it is even more important that the whole company's processes, stories and behaviours support this approach. (See Chapter 8.)

Create customer-centric propositions

This step is critical and frequently the most challenging. For many, it involves looking at what the business does in a completely different light. For example a high-precision engineering business may pride itself on well-engineered products. Sales material is likely to support this product-centric view. It will explain in detail about what the business does and the specifications of particular products. In fact, these businesses are often so focused on their technical excellence and products that all their sales material boasts about these characteristics and not how the customers will use the product. Customers may care about the quality of the product – but they care far more about what it means for them.

What customers truly care about are their own problems. So how does this product or service solve them? Let's use a UK rail company as an example. Different privatized rail transport companies see their businesses differently. They either see their purpose as moving trains from place to place rapidly and efficiently or as a business that satisfies customers' needs for comfortable, reliable transportation between two locations. In the first case, efficient movement of trains is the overriding objective in designing processes and company procedure. Other factors such as train length, timetables and the internal conditions of rolling stock might be sacrificed in order to achieve train movement quotas.

On the other hand, a train company taking a customer-centric view would be less concerned with measuring the movement and number of trains from place to place. It would focus instead on individual customer needs – providing the appropriate rolling stock in a timely fashion and holding spare stock to cater for broken-down and cancelled trains. If the bulk of its regular customers were commuters, it would not decide to delay commuter trains in order to let freight trains move along the line. It might even hold spare stock at key stations and have sufficient back-up staff 'on call' to supply an alternative service when scheduled trains break down or when a driver becomes ill. These actions might increase costs, but they would also significantly improve customer service.

In the first scenario, customers are secondary to the movement of trains; in fact, their demands could be seen as minor nuisances. In the second scenario, the same trains, drivers, etc, could be redeployed with a more customer-centric focus in which trains were provided to provide a safe, comfortable and timely journey between two locations.

This is a critical shift in perspective – from a company's view to a customer's view.

Hospital bed manufacturer

In discussions with customers, the company's sales professionals used to lead with the product's features and benefits. This included their bed being the most manoeuvrable on the market. Customers liked this but the company's conversations with cost-constrained hospitals still came back to price against other bed manufacturers.

The company decided to adopt an insight-led approach, so it could talk to more senior decision makers, earlier in the process. Through research, it found that nurse absence rates and staff turnover were among hospitals' biggest issues, with back pain being a major cause of both. Hospital executives recognized the problem but often did not know the costs or look for a solution.

The company calculated the full impact, which included the costs of temporary staff, sick pay, higher medical insurance rates, hiring and induction time. It then taught hospitals that the true cost was much higher than they thought, so the hospitals realized the need to act. The company then demonstrated that requiring nurses to lift less would reduce back pain and result in major cost savings.

The hospitals could now see a solution but not how to achieve it. The company's sales conversations continued to the point where it was appropriate to highlight the product's differentiators and how they made it easier for nurses to lift and move patients, significantly reducing the chance of back pain. The hospitals were enlightened on a business issue and presented with a solution, with substantial financial and human resources benefits.

By solving a strategically important issue, the bed company is now able to engage HR and finance directors, while its competition can still only address the procurement function.

A cardboard box manufacturer

A leading cardboard box manufacturer serves fast-moving consumer goods (FMCG) companies, who buy boxes to package the goods they sell to retailers. Its customers' purchasing departments treated boxes as a commodity, with price-led decisions being the norm.

The box manufacturer's differentiator was a unique just-in-time ordering system, which customers could install in their warehouses and distribution points. Using this meant that FMCG customers would never have to turn down unexpected orders from large supermarkets, as they would always have enough boxes to fulfil demand.

The box manufacturer's sales conversations majored on its box quality, delivery and the option of using just-in-time ordering. However, its customers' aggressive purchasing departments still focused primarily on price, so the box manufacturer repeatedly lost deals to lower-cost rivals.

The company moved to an insight-led approach and took the time to truly understand its customers. Through both customer and internal research, which included interviewing employees involved in implementation and box delivery, it discovered that FMCG companies kept many surplus boxes in their warehouses. This was driven by fear of being unable to meet demand from the dominant food retailers. Many of these boxes were never used, as they were either damaged over time or became redundant due to changes in packaging requirements. The surplus boxes also took up costly warehouse space.

The box manufacturer calculated the true cost of wastage, floor space and the capital tied up in the surplus boxes, across the hundreds of warehouses that each customer operated, establishing that its customers had a significant working capital issue that they were unaware of. This insight gave the company a powerful reason to talk to its customers' senior finance executives.

By establishing itself as a trusted advisor to directors, the box manufacturer moved its relationship beyond procurement. Its sales conversations now involved working capital improvement, rather than cardboard boxes, and its customers made purchasing decisions based on business value, not lowest price.

Choose the right sales approach(es)

While there are a variety of selling styles, there are only two basic approaches: 1) transactional selling; and 2) consultative selling.

To recap, transactional selling tends to focus on price, key product/ service features and delivery terms. The salesperson qualifies hard to determine whether the prospective customer has a need for the product or service being offered and then tries to close the business. In larger deals and/or big customers, there may be many steps to this process, but it is essentially a simple process: qualify, sell and close.

Consultative selling starts earlier in the customer's buying process. The salesperson first identifies the customer need or opportunity and then helps the customer to define and develop that need into a solution. Selling consists of doing all the things the customer requests, solving the customer problem together with the customer, and then closing the deal.

Transactional selling is appropriate for the bottom half of the Value Pyramid™ while consultative selling is more appropriate for the top two tiers.

Transactional selling

At the lower levels of the Value Pyramid™ – Components and Offers – customers believe that they know what they want and they expect the salesperson to communicate the value (price, delivery, attributes) of the desired commodity. The sales style is 'transactional'. Transactional salespeople qualify hard because they have only well-defined offerings to sell and the potential customer will either need the offerings, or not. Typically, qualifying questions will focus on:

- Need: does the prospective customer believe he/she needs this item and can he/she be convinced of the need?
- Budget: can and will the prospective customer pay for the offering?
- Decision-making process: is the salesperson speaking to the decision maker? How will the decision be made and who will make it? Can the salesperson gain access to the decision maker?
- Competition: who else is after the business? How will the prospective customer decide between vendors?

Some transactional salespeople try to move up the Value Pyramid™ by aggregating products and services and calling the resulting offering a Solution. However, if he or she is still selling to the same person within the customer organization and using the same sales techniques, what is being sold is not a Solution. It is very difficult, almost impossible, for a lone salesperson to sell a true Solution when representing a business whose products are positioned near the bottom of the Value Pyramid™.

These types of misalignment occur all the time in companies. An example of salespeople trying to sell Solutions in a business with a transactional sales mindset occurs when trying to negotiate international deals. Such a salesperson might propose to a global customer a single price based on global use of a product or service, with the overall contract being extremely advantageous in terms of revenue and profit to the selling organization. However, P&L and ultimate control of contracts might be held by country-level managing directors; while in some countries the deal would be great, for others they might end up selling at a loss when applying these terms. So, while the overall organization wins, a few countries might lose. This organizational set-up would conspire against the salesperson closing such a deal because one or two (out of 30 or 40) country managers would veto it. As a result, the overall business would lose.

Another common organizational barrier to the move to consultative solution selling occurs in technical and/or engineering organizations that manufacture and sell by product line. In some cases, there may be some functional overlap between products – a situation that creates competition within the business. Often these businesses give P&L responsibility to manufacturing/development product lines and these business centres drive how sales are contracted. In such business environments it is virtually impossible for a lone salesperson, even a sales manager, to configure a cross-P&L deal where one service line has a higher margin than another.

Sounds silly, doesn't it? The whole business loses out on opportunities because of the way in which the company is structured. Nonetheless, it is a very common occurrence. It takes the commitment and determination of top executives to drive this kind of change. That is why, for solution selling, the whole approach must be top down and supported by processes, appropriate behaviours and collateral from the whole business.

Furthermore, marketing messages and support materials should focus on solving a customer's big issue or opportunity rather than pushing a product or service by citing features and specifications. Top-down selling must employ a consultative approach and sell directly to the senior business person who actually owns the issue. Transactional salespeople often cannot reach this individual and, when they do, their transactional style is usually ineffective. So it is no good just telling an unsupported transactional salesperson to just call on the executive instead of procurement – these individuals will enter the engagement unarmed, speaking the wrong language and displaying the wrong behaviours.

Consultative selling

In this type of selling, the salesperson first engages with the potential customer at an earlier stage in the buying cycle: often at the point when the buyer is only aware of a problem or issue, but has no idea how to solve it or what to buy. The salesperson then has to help the potential customer to clearly articulate the issue or opportunity and work with him/her to create or design a Solution. In contrast to a transactional salesperson, the key skills of a consultative salesperson include:

- knowledge of the customer's industry;
- knowledge of the customer's company;
- ability to lead the customer through the sales process;
- knowledge of the consultative sales process and how it differs from transactional selling.

In addition, these individuals should be empathetic listeners and good at creative problem solving while building a relationship – not just brokering a deal.

Getting the best of both worlds

Businesses that adopt a top-down approach and sell solutions can still sell the component parts and, as a result, they can have the best of both worlds. When businesses wish to sell either business solutions or the component parts, they must develop a consistent marketing strategy and marketing messages to enable them to position their business successfully. In addition, many companies that elect to sell with both selling approaches to appropriate levels of the Value Pyramid™ often use the different salespeople to do the different sales jobs. Why? Not only are the attributes and skills different, but the customer has different expectations of each.

Frequently, it is not a salesperson's skills that let down the business; it is a misalignment of sales approach and perceived value by customers that hinders a company from fully capitalizing on value proposition and customer experience work.

What happens when a business decides to sell some items as Commodity and some as Solutions? Or, as is more common, the business decides to sell transactionally to one segment of the market and consultatively to only a few selected customers? Typically, businesses employ two different sales forces or use distributors or value-added resellers to sell to the commodity segment. There are many options: what is important is that businesses should not restrict themselves to a single sales style when they operate at different levels of the Value Pyramid™ (see Figure 4.2).

The airline industry, for example, has customers ranging from individuals to travel agents to large corporations. In this market, the airlines try to deal with individuals (high-volume transaction, single transaction,

Figure 4.2   Summary sales approach

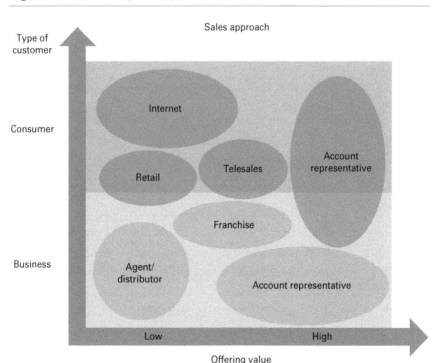

SOURCE Howard, 2014

low-value transactions) via low-cost channels such as the internet. Corporate sales, on the other hand, would be handled by a direct sales force, and large customers would have key account managers.

All key functions and processes, as well as business behaviours, have an impact and should be re-evaluated after value proposition work, especially sales approaches and behaviours.

In Chapter 5, we highlight some of the key differences between consultative and transactional selling and the skills necessary to sell anything.

Frame the sales proposition in the right story

Stories provide a foundation for shared context and verification of mutual perspective between the salesperson, the company and its customers. The crafting of the sales proposition within the sales story is a crucial part of the sales process. See Chapter 6 for detailed information on this topic.

Make sure that everything you do supports your sales propositions

It is not enough for sales staff and sales channels to be geared up to support your new sales propositions: everyone who deals with customers needs to be on board. Otherwise all the good work can easily be undone. Business areas that also need to think differently about how they work and behave include:

- customer service;
- marketing;
- technical support;
- delivery staff;
- accounts;
- receptionists, PAs, secretaries;
- senior management.

In Chapter 8, we explore this need for broader organizational change in more detail.

Case studies: value propositions to sales propositions

CASE STUDY National Vehicle Distribution (NVD)

Irish vehicle distribution company NVD built on Value Proposition Builder™ and Value Pyramid™ work to create a successful new sales proposition. This example illustrates how it followed the eight-step process we have just outlined.

1 Understand what customers value

As part of its value proposition work, NVD identified four core characteristics that its customers valued:

- forward thinking;
- seamless delivery;
- industry leadership;
- relationship building.

2 Understand how they see you

As a next step, NVD assessed where its customers positioned it on the Value Pyramid™. Management found that all its offerings sat firmly in the bottom half: they agreed that commercial discussions were mostly focused on price and delivery time, both of which are attributes of commodity positioning. They did not question this because they understood this type of negotiation is very much in the 'comfort zone' for car dealerships and distributors. Could these customers engage in a different sort of negotiation process? And what could NVD offer them that they might buy in a different way?

3 Identify your core skills and capabilities

Management analysed NVD's core skills, assets and capabilities, listing the most important as:

- trucks;
- drivers;
- logistics systems;

- tracking systems;
- vehicle storage facilities – both dockside and centrally;
- vehicle repair and customization facilities;
- company culture.

NVD invests a great deal of time, effort and money in delivering each of these services in the most high-quality and cost-effective way possible. At this point it is worth noting that the items listed all have 'product-focused' descriptions: they do not yet refer to the value that they provide for customers.

4   Decide where to place propositions on the Value Pyramid™

All the characteristics identified by customers during the value proposition work (forward thinking, seamless delivery, industry leadership and relationship building) suggest a Solutions positioning on the Value Pyramid™. This outcome implies that NVD is well positioned to attempt to shift to a higher-value market position because its customers already believe that it exhibits good leadership and competency. A business with these characteristics is a powerful partner. Yet customers viewed NVD's offerings as commodity items, concentrating almost exclusively on price and delivery times.

5   Create customer-centric propositions

First, NVD's senior team had to ask themselves: what could provide greater value to dealers and distributors? What would customers like to do that they cannot do today? In the past, NVD simply gave new features and products to its customers as part of the service. It was difficult to help customers understand the value of these extras because in its domestic market NVD was by far the largest supplier of vehicle distribution services, so customers had no readily available benchmarks. NVD could have exploited this position and (like some UK rail companies, for example) focused on its own business and cost efficiencies at the expense of customers. Instead, it placed customer service at the core of its delivery, but failed to show domestic customers that they were receiving a world-class service.

In most countries, the various steps in transporting vehicles from factory to dealer are all contracted separately to multiple providers. As a result, the incidence of damage to vehicles is much higher than in Ireland, where one provider is responsible for the whole process. With a single provider, timing from port to end dealer is also much faster, and there is an increased possibility of locating individual cars and expediting selected deliveries. This high level of service has become the norm for Irish dealers. They value it highly but do not pay the extra that it might cost in other countries. Dealers also felt 'trapped' because although NVD's service was excellent, they felt they had no choice in what they bought.

The usual commercial transaction undertaken by dealers was to pay for a vehicle customs clearance, storage, repair and customization (if required), and delivery to the dealer destination. No matter what changes NVD implemented, dealers would still require some combination of these services.

So the challenge for NVD was how to give its customers choice and offer added-value services without impacting business as usual.

After discussions and IT development, NVD developed an added-value service called 'Dealer Track', software that enabled dealers to query the location of any particular car that had left the manufacturing plant. Instead of giving this away as part of their offer, NVD decided to sell it separately after an introductory period of free use. Now, NVD had something for existing customers at several Value Pyramid™ levels.

6   Choosing the right sales approaches

Until this point, selling had consisted of negotiating over price. Introducing a new add-on solution – 'Dealer Track' – would be a departure from this approach.

7   Framing the sales proposition in the right story

The next big challenge was: what to say to current customers and how and who should introduce this new offering. The answer was to allow customers to buy and negotiate as they had previously, while, in addition, offering the new service as an option – without breaking down the components or using it as a negotiating lever for the commodity price list. This solution introduces change slowly, but it does separate the price list items from the new offering. This separation is very important: the new, higher-value offering should be seen as something very different in the customers' minds and they should feel as though they are given a choice about buying it.

8   Make sure that everything you do supports this sales approach

Creating a new service is the first step. The next is to examine current customer touch points and see if other processes needed to be changed. Let's look at the possible impact of the new 'Dealer Track' service. On the one hand, when dealers now know exactly where a car is in the delivery system, this might decrease the number of phone calls to NVD customer service. On the other, the number of calls requesting 'expedited' service might increase. Should NVD therefore add another service, say 'Quick Dealer', to provide exception expediting of individual cars? What would the demand be and how could they deliver it without disrupting regular deliveries? Because new services can have knock-on effects, it is always important to look at them holistically.

CASE STUDY Aircom

Now part of TEOCO, which acquired it in 2013, Aircom International was the market leader in end-to-end network planning and sharing tools and optimization for IP and cellular networks. Over half the world's mobile operators used its products to improve network coverage and quality for over 1.1 billion mobile subscribers worldwide.

The issue

Aircom had been seeing sales reduce by around 8 per cent yearly. Despite having commissioned nine research studies over the past five years to explore why, the decline was accelerating. The company had tried a number of tactical initiatives, to little effect:

- annual sales team reorganizations and new sales director hires;
- new pricing models;
- sales training programmes;
- redesigning marketing and sales materials.

Director of Strategy and Transformation Phil Blades then took a different approach. He commissioned a value proposition design process founded on ethnographic and phenomenological research and observation work among customers and employees. This approach provided important insights into Aircom's problems.

Market insights

The research showed that only strategic innovation could deal with the long-term (5- to 10-year horizon) trends that were buffeting the telecom industry. Over-the-top (OTT) apps like iMessage, which could bypass the networks of mobile operators, were hitting operators' revenues; consumer expectations were constantly rising and technology change was accelerating.

Customers were looking for a more collaborative, 'business partner' approach from suppliers to help them address these challenges. It was becoming apparent that to sustain margins in the long term, suppliers needed to become more than just providers of products and tools.

The big picture

Figure 4.3   Telecoms value chain

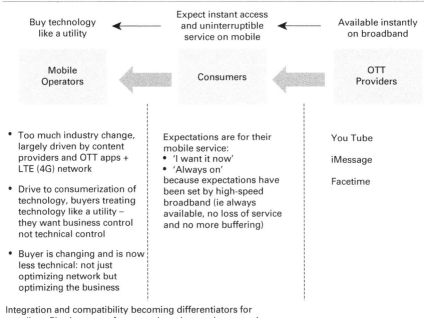

Buy technology like a utility ◄——— Expect instant access and uninterruptible service on mobile ◄——— Available instantly on broadband

| Mobile Operators | ⬅ Consumers ⬅ | OTT Providers |

- Too much industry change, largely driven by content providers and OTT apps + LTE (4G) network

- Drive to consumerization of technology, buyers treating technology like a utility – they want business control not technical control

- Buyer is changing and is now less technical: not just optimizing network but optimizing the business

Expectations are for their mobile service:
- 'I want it now'
- 'Always on' because expectations have been set by high-speed broadband (ie always available, no loss of service and no more buffering)

You Tube

iMessage

Facetime

Integration and compatibility becoming differentiators for suppliers. Plus increase of managed services and outsourcing

Aircom had other, short-term issues that were revealed by the research:

- While individual products were good, they had not been bundled or packaged well, and they were not helping operators to grow their businesses.

- The company's approach was rational – focused on technical expertise, tools and skilled people, and promoting benefits around productivity, cost saving and security. However, its customers placed a higher value on emotional factors, such as the frequency of meetings and the depth of relationships. This trend was noticeable in specific countries – and it was in these countries where sales were falling most.

- Real competition came from the customer buyer, who was taking control of the network optimization journey.

Using the Value Proposition Builder™ methodology (see Chapter 3), Aircom built its Value Proposition Blueprint™ using four elements (Figure 4.4):

- customers' emotional value drivers;
- customers' rational value drivers;

Figure 4.4 Aircom Value Proposition Blueprint™

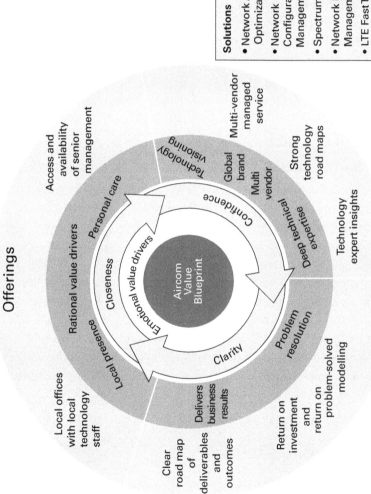

Offerings

Access and
availability
of senior
management

Personal care

Technology
visioning

Multi-vendor
managed
service

Rational value drivers

Closeness

Confidence

Global
brand

Multi
vendor

Strong
technology
road maps

Emotional value drivers

Aircom
Value
Blueprint

Deep technical
expertise

Technology
expert insights

Local presence

Problem
resolution

Clarity

Local offices
with local
technology
staff

Delivers
business
results

Clear
road map
of
deliverables
and
outcomes

Return on
investment
and
return on
problem-solved
modelling

Solutions

- Network Audit and
  Optimization
- Network
  Configuration
  Management
- Spectrum Refarming
- Network Performance
  Management
- LTE FastTrack

SOURCE Futurecurve, 2016

- offerings;
- solutions.

The emotional drivers identified by the research were particularly important:

- Closeness: Aircom was good at this. It had people on the ground in local offices, even at a remote location in Afghanistan. Its staff understood local culture and customers had access to senior people, not just technical staff, at Aircom locations around the world.
- Clarity: this was an area for improvement. Customers wanted to be clear about business cases and outcomes and wanted to understand how projects would be implemented with a clear ROI.
- Confidence: customers needed to feel their technology was future-proof and that Aircom was going to continue supporting and implementing the best tools. Again, Aircom needed to work harder in this area.

Aircom's sales propositions

Using this process together with its value proposition framework, Aircom grouped together new solutions to focus on its customers' priority areas. It re-emphasized benefits, taking into account emotional issues such as local culture and personal service.

It painted a picture for its customers of the high-level industry drivers, the customers' specific drivers and how customers – and Aircom – fitted into this bigger picture. Aircom then explained how it could help customers to achieve their long-term goals in this context. This approach was a radical departure from its previous approach to sales propositions, and it reframed what the company did.

One new sales proposition was 'spectrum refarming'. Aircom created LTE Fast Track to ensure the migration to 4G was more cost-effective for operators by enabling them to use their current spectrum. Aircom also offered this capability as a managed service.

Here's how Aircom told the customer story:

LTE Fast Track Managed Service

Many operators find it both difficult and expensive to manage and optimize networks so they run smoothly and securely and accommodate new migrations without any downtime. It requires ongoing investment in hardware and software, endless updates, new staff hires and staff training.

Most operators contract with many vendors, all of whom optimize different parts of the network with different tools. Our research has shown that managing more than six different vendors who all use different tools will increase your management time by an average of 67 per cent and raise purchasing costs by 32 per cent. Both time and costs increase exponentially as you add more vendors.

This is where managed services come in. A managed service provider has the expertise and equipment to optimize and monitor your network and deliver applications efficiently and safely. And instead of requiring upfront capital expenditures, managed services let you shift all network management costs from capital expenditure to the operational side, paying for what you actually use (instead of what someone thinks you might need). Managed services let the customer free up internal resources to work on more strategic issues that relate directly to your core business.

Using multivendor toolsets, Aircom's managed service gives you all this with an average 37 per cent reduction on your purchase costs and reduction in network downtime of up to 62 per cent.

The sales propositions for each customer group and for different solutions from Aircom now had a different story, a different emphasis and priority of messages within the story. Most importantly, the story was now based on truth and on what customers actually experienced and wanted.

It now focused on helping the customers to migrate and grow their business; the things that were important to the customer and in line with their strategic objectives rather than purely offering tools that could do a particular job of optimizing a network. Their value proposition and related sales propositions now displayed a richness that had been previously lacking, articulated in the customer's language. As a consequence of these changes, sales from both new and existing customers increased by 16 per cent in just one geographical area within the first year.

The value proposition to sales proposition illustrated in this case study relates to just one of the sales propositions that Aircom was able to create for one specific customer target group. Each clearly defined customer target group required a specific sales proposition based on the behaviours and worldview of each customer group.

Sales propositions can be developed on their own. However, they are at their most powerful when they are created from a total value proposition, so both are important. Figure 4.5 shows how sales propositions flow from value propositions.

Figure 4.5 Your value proposition gives you the design framework for how you want your customers to buy once they have made contact

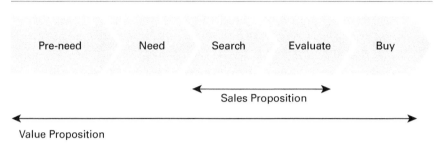

The value proposition gives you the design framework for how you want your customers to engage with and experience your company. Sales propositions and their accompanying stories help them buy once they have made contact.

As sales propositions need to be created at the product, service or customer level, a company may need to generate a good number of them. Developing the total value proposition provides the framework for generating those sales propositions and gives an organization the capability to do so. Such sales propositions will also be consistent with each other and with a company's overall strategic positioning, ensuring coherent communication. Therefore, creating your total value proposition first gives you one version of your company truth that is drawn from your customer truth, and one master blueprint from which all your sales propositions and stories can emerge.

This framework saves huge amounts of expense and effort, including the time and resources of your salespeople, marketing staff, internal communications and product people, who otherwise end up creating multiple 'truths' for multiple purposes.

As well as helping your sales and marketing people to be more effective, defining your value proposition first can also significantly reduce marketing agency spending by ensuring that a company has the right customer-validated and researched content from the start. Insights can also feed back into the overall value proposition, allowing the business to refine and strengthen it.

Self-test: value proposition or sales proposition?

You can use the following set of statements to determine whether a value proposition or sales proposition is best for your current needs. Are you mostly concerned with the statement in column **A** or column **B**?

	A	Select A or B	B
1	Defining the intended customer experience for your customers in terms of their needs and expectations from your business and aligning all teams to understand and deliver this customer experience		Ensuring the customer experience of the sales and marketing process meets customer expectations and is a positive reflection of the company brand
2	Developing persuasive stories that can be used at any level including the company, divisions or business units, customer sectors or segments, persona or buyer type		Creating persuasive stories that are used for an individual customer or prospect at an opportunity level
3	Understanding the main market challenges facing your key customer groups so that you can respond to the following questions: 'How can you give us competitive advantage?' 'Why should I consider your company?' 'Why should I consider your offering?'		Answering the customer's key buying questions of: 'Why should I change from what I have now to a new offering?' 'Why should I buy from you rather than another company?' 'Why should I buy now?'

	A	Select A or B	B
4	Configuring and positioning your portfolio of offerings: products, services and solutions at the company level, division or business unit level, customer sector or segment level, persona or buyer type level		Repackaging and bundling the portfolio of offerings: products, services and solutions, at the individual customer or prospect level and/or at an opportunity level
5	Assessing your customer's alternative options and substitutes to using you. (Looking beyond your traditional competitors.) Identifying precisely how you are different from and better than each of these options.		The sales team's understanding of the customer's perceived risks of buying from you. Their ability to differentiate your offerings appropriately for a customer or prospect, considering the range of alternative and substitute options to the customer.

If you have scored:

- Mostly **A**s: you need to develop your customer-centric total value proposition.

- 50/50 **A** and **B**: you need to develop both, starting with your overarching value proposition.

- Mostly **B**s: you need to develop your customer-centric sales proposition.

References

Christensen, Clayton M and Raynor, Michael E. (2003) *The Innovator's Solution*, Harvard Business School Publishing Corporation, Boston

Christensen Institute, The (2016) [accessed 23 November 2016] Jobs To Be Done [Online] http//www.christenseninstitute.org/jobs-to-be-done/

Howard, Tamara (2014) *Who's Paying for Lunch?*, Verve Business Books Ltd, Oxfordshire

The sales process

05

Many readers of this book will be familiar with the sales process, the sales cycle and the different types of selling. If you are one of these readers, we would suggest you skip this chapter and move on to read about sales storytelling in Chapter 6, a summary of our Laws of Value Proposition Selling in Chapter 7, or 'Creating the selling organization' in Chapter 8.

If, on the other hand, you are relatively new to the nuances of selling, you may find this chapter useful. In order to properly exploit your sales proposition it is important to understand each stage of the sales cycle from both the salesperson's and the customer's perspective.

Stages of the sales process

A quick review of the standard sales process shows what is happening at each stage:

- to progress the sale;
- to show what is going on in the mind of the customer;
- and to illustrate the different activities of the two sales types mentioned so far.

The circular diagram in Figure 5.1 illustrates the process for any type of sales opportunity and for all types of sales approaches. In large organizations many of these processes may be occurring simultaneously as different sales opportunities arise and customer needs are met. For new customers, the first sales engagement may start as early as the 'suspect' stage.

Figure 5.1   The eight steps of the sales process

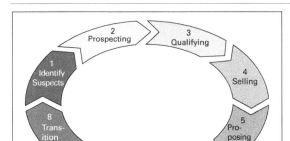

The sales process maps the stages of successfully selling and closing an 'opportunity'

- More than one step may happen within one sales meeting
- Some steps may take many sales meetings to complete
- You may be at different stages with different opportunities within the same customer

SOURCE Verve Consulting, 2016

Many organizations use these terms loosely without consideration for what each means in terms of what is going on in a prospective customer's mind and what a salesperson should be doing. This process is appropriate for *any* sales process for any type of business – from consumer retail to large, complex B2B sales – the key differences are how much time is spent in each stage and some of the techniques for moving the process forward. The key role of any salesperson is to successfully and efficiently move the customer from stage to stage until a contract is signed and the offering delivered. For simplicity's sake, the descriptions below will speak about 'new business' but these rules apply just as well to new opportunities with an existing customer.

What is happening at each stage of the cycle?

Suspects

Let's start at the beginning: suspects. Suspects are merely an aggregation or segmentation of businesses, whether by geography or business type, where there might be a business opportunity. For example, new business salespeople are often given a geographic area in which to sell and, until every company is 'qualified', everyone on the patch is a potential customer. Of course it would be inefficient for the salesperson to ring every company; there are quicker ways to identify good companies. Ideally, salespeople do not focus on suspects – these individuals would be too expensive a resource to just knock on doors without a good reason. Typically, the marketing department creates campaigns aimed at suspects – for example, social media bursts, mailshots, advertising, seminars – in order to isolate good prospects.

> So what's going on in a suspect's mind at this stage?
> – 'I don't know I have a problem/need' or 'I don't know your business exists.'

So, neither consultative nor transactional salespeople should be deployed to chase suspects – it is a waste of resources.

Prospects

Prospects are individuals or businesses that are known to have an interest in a company's offering. It is at this stage that a salesperson makes contact to determine whether the interest is real.

In the case of *transactional* salespeople, the questions and the buyers within the organization are straightforward:

- Does the prospective customer have a budget?
- When and how does the company plan to make a purchase?
- How will the decision to buy be made?

These are all qualifying questions that the salesperson should ask in order to turn the prospect into a qualified prospect. This description makes qualifying sound easy and, in some cases, it is. However, in others the initial contact may be someone who is merely 'shopping' on behalf of a potential buyer, so the salesperson will need to uncover this relationship and try to gain access to the ultimate decision maker.

The buyer is typically either a procurement professional or a mid-level, departmental manager with a fixed solution in mind.

What's going on in a prospect's mind at this stage?

'I buy something similar to your product (but not from you), but...
I didn't know you existed or could help me.'

'I have misconceptions about your product or company.'

'I don't have a good reason to move from my current supplier.'

In the case of *consultative* salespeople, while the objective of this phase is the same, the buyer and the questions are slightly different.

- Does the prospective customer have a burning issue or want to exploit a business opportunity?
- Is there any time pressure on the prospective customer to 'do something' soon?
- Can the selling company put together a solution to solve the issue/exploit the opportunity?
- How much is it worth to the buying business? What is the value to the individual who owns the problems?
- How will a decision to proceed be made?
- Who will make the final decision and does anyone else need to be involved?

The buyer is the business person who owns the problem or opportunity.

What's going on in a prospect's mind at this stage?

'You sound like you know what you are talking about and have some experience solving my issue or exploiting similar opportunities, but... I didn't know you could help me.'

'How can I be sure your company will do what you say?'

'How can I convince my business peers that working with your company is the best option?'

'How can I minimize the risk to my business of choosing you or your solution?'

Qualified prospect

By the stage of the qualified prospect, two important things should have occurred if the opportunity is worth pursuing. First, the prospect is now aware that the selling company offers a particular product, service or solution. Second, the salesperson now understands the prospect's needs, budget, time frame and how a decision will be made. It is at this point that the salesperson can begin to sell in earnest or qualify-out the opportunity and not pursue the sale.

By now, in the *transactional selling* situation, the qualified prospect is thinking:

'I buy a product similar to one you sell', and...

'I know you exist and believe you have a product I could buy.'

'And we have agreed what you need to do to convince me to buy from you.'

In the *consultative selling* situation, the qualified prospect is typically cautiously excited. If successful, the salesperson has demonstrated a good understanding of the business environment in which this business operates and can bring the selling company's experience to bear on solving the issues.

What this individual is thinking:

'I hope the salesperson is right. If so, it would be a load off my mind!'

'How can I quickly assess whether to buy, so that if this solution works I can use it for my business as quickly as possible?'

So, in both these instances, by the time a salesperson has reached the qualified prospect stage the target company should know all about the selling company. Knowing that a particular company exists, and understanding the full range of its capabilities, is a very important step. No one can buy from a company if he or she doesn't know the company or its offerings. Many smaller businesses or those trying to break into new markets may not get asked to bid for opportunities because no one in the prospect's company has heard of them.

This problem can often be even worse for large, well-recognized brands selling to existing customers.

Why? Well, many reasons and, typically, all of them are found together in large corporations. Most large corporations organize their business in a siloed fashion with multiple sales forces and marketing functions. Such large corporations are myopic and focus more on their own organizations than their customers', so a value proposition analysis can be a shock to them. In any case, this short-sightedness results in poor communications to the market.

For large customers of these siloed businesses, there may be many salespeople selling different offerings to the same or different departments in the customer business. Often, there is also an account management or relationship management function thrown into the mix as well. With this confusing mix of individuals, the prospect can hear mixed messages or, in some cases, mishear about some of the offerings. He or she may not ask about an offering out of ignorance – and such ignorance is not the fault of the customer! Careful qualifying of all potential opportunities would uncover these situations. Once uncovered, the appropriate salesperson can then engage in selling activity.

It is worth summarizing at this point what is happening in the customer journey thus far and what the salesperson should be facilitating (see Figure 5.2).

Before moving on to the next stage, it is also worth summarizing what sales activities should be carried out at each of the first three stages (see Figure 5.3).

After thorough qualification, should the salesperson or selling team decide to proceed, the next step is to move into the selling phase of the cycle (see Figure 5.4).

Figure 5.2 The customer journey so far

The eight steps of the sales process

- 2 Prospecting
- 3 Qualifying
- 1 Identify Suspects
- 4 Selling
- 8 Transition
- 5 Proposing
- 7 Contracting
- 6 Closing

- Educate the prospect – make him/her knowledgeable about your company and its products
- Begin to build trust by questioning and listening
- Make him/her feel comfortable and happy to speak with you
- By the end of qualifying, make him/her want more....

SOURCE Verve Consulting, 2016

Figure 5.3 Prospect issues and sales activities

What do you need to do to put the customer at ease?

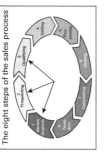

The eight steps of the sales process

What's going on:
Prospect/Customer issues

Identify suspect	↗ 'I don't know I have a problem/need' or 'I don't know you exist'
Prospecting	↗ 'I buy something similar to your product (but not from you), but... I don't know you exist.' Or 'I have misconceptions about your product or company.' Or 'I don't have a good reason to move from my current supplier.'
Qualifying	↗ 'I buy a product similar to one you sell and I know you exist and believe you have a product I could buy.'
	PLUS
	'We have agreed what you need to do to convince me to buy from you.'

What you need to do:
Sales activities

Identify suspects	↗ 1. Determine whether this company uses anything you sell and can afford to buy your product. Typically done via marketing.
Prospecting	↗ 1. Confirm that this company/individual uses something you sell. Often done via marketing and 'cold calling'.
	2. Confirm that he/she knows that your company offers the product.
	3. Determine what it would take to get him/her to move from current supplier.
	4. Make certain the prospect doesn't have bad feelings or misconceptions about your company. Give the company your 'General Benefits Statement'.
Qualifying	↗ 1. Uncover any 'killer concerns'.
	2. Determine price sensitivity.
	3. Who will take the decision? Will other people be involved? If yes, who? And is there a process that must be followed?
	4. Is there a time dependency or delivery urgency?
	5. What would it take to get him/her to change?
	6. Determine specs and quantities of current usage.
	7. 'Trial close'.

SOURCE Verve Consulting, 2016

Figure 5.4 Moving sales along

Examples of what to do to move things along

Sales stage	Actions	For example:
Suspect → Prospect	Confirm that suspect actually has need for product	1. Various marketing programmes 2. Cold call (not very efficient!)
Prospect → Qualified Prospect	Confirm that prospect has money and need and that he/she knows you supply	1. Do mailshot with feedback card 2. Collect names from: current customers, 'customer's customers', employees who come from competitors, website enquiries, etc. 3. Cold call

Qualified Prospect → Begin selling	Understand what it would take to get the prospect to buy from you – Get the Who? When? How? How much?	1. Meet the prospect/customer
		2. Discuss the opportunity and understand all the details around current purchasing needs:
		  • Where buying now?
		  • Who makes the procurement decision?
		  • Who else is involved in making the decision?
		  • What is the customer paying now?
		  • What are the specs?
		  • Is the customer/prospect completely happy with current supplier or have there been issues?

IT IS AT THIS STAGE THAT <u>YOU</u> MIGHT UNCOVER A 'KILLER CONCERN' AND DECIDE NOT TO PURSUE THIS OPPORTUNITY

SOURCE Verve Consulting, 2016

Selling

The 'selling' stage consists of those activities agreed between the salesperson and the prospective customer during the qualifying stage. Paraphrasing the conversation, what should have been established is who needs to be convinced and how, in order for the prospective customer to agree to buy. The selling phase consists of going through these steps with all the appropriate individuals. There are skills involved in managing this phase correctly, but the process is straightforward. For the selling company, the single most costly mistake in the sales process is moving into this phase *without proper qualification*. Many companies and salespeople are worried about taking an opportunity off a prospective sales list (sales funnel) so carry on with the process and waste time, resources and money that could be better deployed selling to someone who would buy something. Critical analysis here is vital to assess whether to qualify-out of the sale at this stage.

So, assuming that the salesperson is now working with a fully qualified prospect, what's happening in the customer's mind during all the sales activity?

What the prospective customer is thinking at this stage is:

'I need to be convinced I am making the right decision.'

'I need my boss/colleagues/the users to be convinced.'

'I want to understand all the risks and feel comfortable about them.'

These thoughts are the same, no matter which sales style is employed. One good practice during this stage is to communicate regularly with the qualified prospects about the sales activities and findings as well as the responses of various colleagues. Keeping the key contact in the loop helps to make him/her feel more in control of the process, and feeling in control gives the prospective customer comfort. Also, if the customer is kept informed of the proposal preparation throughout the process, commenting and adding critical pieces of information, then when the proposal does arrive it will be expected and welcomed because the customer has had input.

This stage can take anything from a few days to a few months or even years, depending on the prospective customer's buying process, what is being sold, and how many individuals need to play a role in the decision making. However, the time frame is usually a few weeks or months. During the selling phase, the salesperson can begin to create the final proposal, which is presented at the next phase.

Proposing

Proposing represents the formal ending of the selling phase and can take many forms: written proposal; letter; and/or formal presentations. In some instances, there may be multiple presentations and proposals or combinations of the two, depending on the size and structure of the buyer organization. By this stage, the salesperson or team should have established a relationship with everyone in the prospective customer who has any role in the decision-making process and 'socialized' the ideas and arguments that will appear in the final proposal. The contents should not be a shock; if sold properly, the buyer should be expecting whatever is written in the contents of the proposal.

At this stage, the prospective customer is thinking:

'I need to understand the rational reason for buying this product from your company.'

'I need to see the options in "black and white".'

Closing

Of course, if a business is genuinely selling, merely proposing and waiting for the customer to buy is not enough. Whoever is in charge of the selling process must 'ask for the business' or 'close'. Although this action sounds obvious, many, many salespeople cannot do it and hope that the customer will ask to buy. While that does happen and the customer is forced to ask to buy, it returns control of the selling process back to the prospective customer and thereby puts the selling company in a less advantageous negotiating position.

When 'closing', what the customer is thinking and feeling is:

'I need to be sure and I have heard and seen everything, that I understand what I will be buying and that I am making the right decision.'

'I need to trust the person and company who is selling to me.'

These thoughts occur in all prospective customers – whether the selling is transactional or consultative.

Negotiating

The negotiating stage occurs when final contracts are discussed and then signed. Negotiation is *not* about whether the customer will buy, because by this stage the customer has already said 'yes'. Rather, negotiating is about the terms – price, quality, delivery, etc – of the purchase.

In practice, a sale must be won (or lost!) three times:

- First, during the qualifying stage when a salesperson asks 'If I could show you the way to… would you buy from me?'
- Second, when the prospective customer says 'yes' to the proposal.
- And finally, when contracts are signed.

A good deal can be lost at any of these stages, if and when the sale process is badly handled.

One big mistake that is frequently made is to begin negotiations too early in the sales process. Negotiating on price or delivery too early reduces the seller's final negotiating leverage at the end of the sales process and negotiation will always occur at this stage. Such a mistake occurs most frequently in a transactional selling environment and when dealing with procurement or purchasing departments. A good salesperson will try to agree to everything else about a deal, in principle, before agreeing on final terms.

> At the negotiation stage, the customer's thoughts tend to be:
>
> 'I need to be certain that I am getting the very best deal.'
>
> 'I don't want to feel like I have been "taken advantage of".'

The negotiation phase tends to play a big role in large, transactional sales deals, but is rarely a big issue after the 'close' of a consultative sale.

Transition

Once contracting is concluded, customers may be subject to 'buyer's remorse'. It is a natural emotional response to surrendering power by agreeing to a business deal. Care should always be taken at this stage to ensure that the customer remains happy with the decision to buy. The emotional elements of the buying/selling process come to the fore at this stage.

> The customer is now thinking:
>
> 'Once I buy, will the company still pay attention to me?'
>
> 'I'm worried that I won't see anyone from Company X now that I've signed on the dotted line.'

Transactional salespeople are typically measured on the signing of a contract so are far more likely to abandon a customer at this stage. Good consultative salespeople tend to manage the transition phase as part of the selling process.

There are many important lessons that may be illustrated by studying the sales process and some can be gleaned from the preceding paragraphs. When properly conducted, the sales process should be managed and led by the salesperson or selling team, not the customer.

Figure 5.5   The customer journey – selling through to delivery

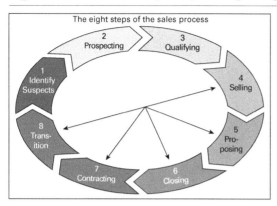

The eight steps of the sales process

2 Prospecting
3 Qualifying
1 Identify Suspects
4 Selling
8 Transition
5 Proposing
7 Contracting
6 Closing

During these stages the customer can feel most vulnerable. Some behaviours that help:

- Acknowledge his/her concerns and deal with them
- Listen and playback what you hear to confirm understanding
- Make certain that the customer has moved to the next sales stage emotionally as well as rationally
- Provide a rational basis to help him/her select your product
- Make him/her feel good about the decision to buy

SOURCE Verve Consulting, 2016

In driving the process, the salesperson should be aware of the rational reasons for buying, but also understand the emotional state of the buyer at each stage. Finally, when selling to large corporations, company politics can play a huge role in who needs to be consulted and how the sales process is driven.

Selling successfully is much more than a verbal, intellectual process. A good salesperson will make key customer contacts *feel* comfortable and must engage with the customer (one or many) in an honest and open exchange and not look away or act embarrassed. A successful salesperson is not apologetic and asks for what he or she wants and asks clearly. Most importantly, every representative from the selling organization should believe what is being said. Customers pick up on this lack of belief and it can erode trust. Finally, it is important that a customer feels 'heard'. Never ignore customer objections.

Objections handling provides an excellent illustration of why a salesperson should understand exactly where he or she is in the selling process. The subtext of objections will often vary with each phase of the process.

Objections can mean different things at different stages of the sales process and provide good clues to a prospective customer's state of mind.

In dealing with objections, knowing the phase of the sales process helps the salesperson to provide the best answer.

Figure 5.6 Later prospect issues and sales activities

The customer journey (selling stages 4, 5 and 6)

The eight steps of the sales process

What's going on:
Prospect/Customer issues

Selling
→ 'I need to be convinced I am making the right decision.'

'I need my boss/colleagues/the users to be convinced.'

'I want to understand all the risks and feel comfortable about them.'

Proposing
→ 'I need to understand the rational reason for buying this product from your company.'

'I need to see the options in "black and white".'

Closing
→ 'I need to be sure that I have heard and seen everything, that I understand what I will be buying and that I am making the right decision.'

'I need to trust your company'

What you need to do:
Sales activities

Selling
→ Meet and sell to everyone on the buyer map.

Collect all the information required by the customer to make his/her decision.

Do any product analysis/technical tests required (and only if necessary).

Proposing
→ Prepare a written document that contains all information necessary to buy your product.

Include everything in the proposal/letter that the customer told you he/she needed in order to make the decision.

Agree and meet the formal date for delivering the proposal (and, if possible, the date for decision).

Closing
→ Sum up your activities so far.

Ask for the business.

SOURCE Verve Consulting, 2016

Table 5.1 The subtext of objections will often vary with each phase of the process

Stage of Sale	What the Customer's Objections at this Stage Indicate They are Thinking
Cold calling, initial meeting	'I don't want to change!'
Qualifying	'I don't trust you yet!'
Selling	'I'm worried I will make a mistake.'
Closing	'I plan to buy from you but I'm still a bit nervous about it.'
Negotiating	'How do I know I'm getting the best deal?

SOURCE Verve Consulting, 2016

The four sales types

The sales process is extremely important. It provides a road map for sales staff to follow and, if done well, can show insights into the customer's state of mind at various stages. All good salespeople follow this process, but how they behave and how much time each spends at various stages will depend on what they sell and to whom they are selling. To gain a clearer picture, it is worth spending a bit of time understanding the different types of salespeople and the different styles of selling that are appropriate to each.

There are basically four types of salesperson:

- transactional;
- expert;
- solution;
- consultative.

Each approach, when done well, is designed to deal with different sales situations and all have some common characteristics:

- good listener;
- knows his/her company's offerings and/or expertise very well;
- personable;
- can ask challenging questions.

If you were looking for the attributes of a good salesperson of any type, you might list: creative, directive, entertaining, instructive or teaching and able to guide others. This is what Matthew Dixon and Brent Adamson explain clearly in their book *The Challenger Sale* (Dixon and Adamson, 2011). In this way, the salesperson can respond to new and challenging situations while educating and guiding a prospect or customer through the sales process. It should feel as though the two – sales and customer – take the sales journey together. So, having said these attributes are the same across all sales types, what is different?

The buying cycle

The simple answer to the above question is that what differs is what the prospective customer is buying and where he or she is in the buying process.

In the buying process, what is driving the prospective customer can range from a distinct malaise or discomfort around how to tackle a business issue or opportunity, to knowing exactly what is needed to solve a recognized and well-understood problem. There are also stages in the middle in which a prospective customer believes he/she has an idea of what to do, but is unclear on all the details. Each of these stages demands a different style of sales approach and a different relationship with the person who is doing the selling. The Value Pyramid™ and market positioning will dictate what sales approach is more appropriate. The rest of Chapter 5 will help illustrate how the sales process can be used to identify the optimum approach.

> 8th Law of Value Proposition Selling: use the sales process as a guide and select the appropriate sales approach and style for your market positioning.

Figure 5.7 illustrates the different stages of the buying cycle, from left to right.

Figure 5.7   Needs-based buying

'Needs'-based buying

What does the customer believe he or she 'needs' to address an issue or opportunity to solve a problem?

STAGE 1	STAGE 2	STAGE 3	STAGE 4
Vague unease, external factors cause concern or speculation **No specific solutions**	Recognizes the problem or opportuntity but doesn't know **what** to do	Think they have a solution and know the 'what' but not the **how**	Knows the 'what' and has a plan for the 'how', needs to figure out **who**

SOURCE Howard, 2014

Starting on the far right, where the buyer knows exactly what he or she needs to buy, transactional selling comes into its own. The salesperson only has a limited range of offerings and needs to assess quickly whether anything fits the prospective customer's requirements. There is very little 'wiggle room' in this situation. These purchases are often made by individuals in procurement who are far removed from the business people who have the issue being addressed. The salesperson's offering either fits or it doesn't. Most successful selling comes down to price, service and determining whether unique product features are important. This situation is ideal for the transactional sales model.

A competent, *transactional* salesperson is very directive and good at trying to uncover needs that map onto his/her offering's unique features. The conversational style is questioning, so as to qualify and guide the prospect or customer to the next stage of the sales cycle. Most of the time and effort is focused on qualifying and closing, and they will race through the selling and proposing stages, doing only the minimum required. It is only a bad transactional salesperson who may try to sell an inappropriate offering when the prospective customer clearly does not have a need.

The next sales type, the *expert* salesperson, is typically a consultant and sells his or her own expertise. The appropriate phase of the buying cycle depends on whether this individual is a content expert – in other words, expert in a very specific field – or a process expert, usually a project or programme manager, or a change manager. These individuals sell most successfully when the buyer is not quite certain about some aspect of a solution or lacks specific technical skill.

A good expert salesperson sells by displaying his/her expertise and generally spends a higher proportion of a meeting with a customer doing the talking than does any other sales type. The objective in talking is to display knowledge and expertise. This type of salesperson rarely closes and, in fact, selling consists of getting the customer to buy from him or her by them asking 'Do you think you could do that for us too?' Qualifying is cruder – the expert talks about his/her area of expertise and the prospective customer either 'bites' or doesn't. Control of the sale is clearly in the hands of the prospect.

This expert approach tends to work when a customer needs only one or two experts and does not lend itself to selling product or a complex solution. A solution salesperson or a consultative salesperson is far better when a customer needs a complex or individually configured solution.

The *solutions* salesperson works best earlier in the buying cycle when a prospective customer is not sure exactly what is needed or how to resolve a business issue. However, different from the transactional salesperson, solutions selling deals directly with the person who owns the issues and has the authority and budget to take actions to solve them. This type of salesperson feels comfortable talking to people in the business, but still approaches them in a sales role.

The sales style employs a directed questioning technique that enables the salesperson to lead the conversation while letting the customer do most of the talking. The objective is to get the customer to elaborate on issues and opportunities so as to latch onto and shape solutions that his/her own company can deliver. To sell in this manner takes a great deal of preparation before interacting with a prospective customer.

How does the salesperson prepare? Typically, the selling company has already gone to the trouble of configuring some outline solutions that can serve as templates in solutions selling. This work is vital in order to provide guideline pricing and positioning. For this style of selling, no solution will be off-the-shelf but there will be building blocks that can be assembled and configured to provide the basis for a proposal. The salesperson should be well versed in the common issues and opportunities facing companies in his/her prospective customer's market niche and feel comfortable taking part in a business discussion. Because of this business orientation, often solutions salespeople focus on selected markets, but are able to sell a broad range of their own company's products and services packaged as a market specific solution. These individuals need to be creative and be able to shape solutions.

The final sales style is *consultative* selling – a term often misunderstood as 'selling consulting', but nothing could be further from the truth. These professionals are closest in type to solutions salespeople. Where possible, they focus very early in the buying cycle on the key decision maker who feels the pain or an issue, or wants to exploit a market opportunity. A prominent difference between the two is that the consultative sales approach is peer-to-peer and conducted by a very senior individual in the selling company. This style is the only approach that works for joint ventures – both parties must be empowered and able to respect the expertise and authority of the other. Clearly, this style works best where a company – or a division of the company – sells few, very large and complex deals.

For large, complex deals, there is yet another sales approach: '*team selling*'. This approach is invariably used in consultative selling situations and the overall sales lead deploys this style. However, the team may consist of many individuals, some of whom are expert salespeople, some are transactional salespeople and some are people who have no sales experience at all. To detail how to employ team selling successfully requires a second book, but what is critical about this approach is that the selling company defines and uses a clear, team selling process with a salesperson in charge of the overall activity. The rest of the team need to understand that, whatever their expertise, they are playing a role in a selling activity and should adjust their usual behaviours accordingly.

An important point for sales meetings is stated in Law 9.

> 9th Law of Value Proposition Selling: you cannot mix your selling styles in one meeting, eg consultative with transactional. For team selling scenarios, you must have a team selling process with clearly delineated roles and responsibilities.

The key lessons from this chapter are:

1 There is a well-defined selling process that all companies should understand and use.

2 Businesses should map all their selling and sales support activities along this process to ensure that all activities work to progress sales engagements to the contracting phase.

3 There are four distinct types of salespeople, each appropriate to different stages in the buying cycle and different sales offerings.

4 Different sales types sell to different individuals in the prospect business and use a different selling style.

An authentic business applies Law 4 of selling your value proposition to all sales opportunities.

4th Law of Value Proposition Selling: sales behaviours must be directed towards helping the customer gain maximum value from your offerings.

Therefore, understanding these sales basics is critical when selling a company's unique value proposition. To do so takes the right people or team, the right process and a common understanding throughout the whole company, of what sales is trying to sell.

Self-test: what is your sales philosophy?

From each pair of descriptive statements (**A** and **B**) note which statement more closely resembles your sales philosophy:

	A	Select A or B	B
1	Focus on revenue and/or volume		Focus on margin and/or profitability
2	Pursue a capacity-driven strategy, eg keep the factory going		Pursue a value-driven strategy, eg focused on solving customer problems
3	Believe customers are only motivated by price		Proactively use insights from customers to improve the value of your offerings

4	Use price concessions and discounts to win business	Flex your approach to match the customer, eg look for the 'win–win' result with collaborative customers but 'take a position' and negotiate hard with the 'hard ball' customer
5	Sell primarily on price comparisons with competitors	Sell primarily on customer total cost of ownership (TCO) comparisons, helping customers assess buying from you versus buying from competitors, (considering the non-traditional options)
6	Gain repeat business by lowering prices	Gain repeat business at the same price or improved margins
7	Give away services for free to close the deal	Use services to generate additional business/ revenues
8	Give price concessions to customers without changing the offering	Give price concessions to customers only in exchange for cost-saving reductions in the offering
9	Offer unsupported claims about value to customers	Provide evidence of superior value to customers
10	Customer experience is a sales and marketing responsibility with no 'back office' accountability	Customer needs and expectations are understood by the whole business and are a positive reflection of the company brand

If you have scored:

- Mostly **A**s: your company is feeling pressurized. You are selling on price not value. Work on your value proposition is imperative.

- 50/50 **A** and **B**: your company has some insight into its value proposition to customers but is missing key elements. Working on your company value proposition will make a material difference to your sales performance.

- Mostly **B**s: your company has a good insight into its value to customers and is doing a good job of selling on value.

References

Dixon, Matthew and Adamson, Brent (2011) *The Challenger Sale: Taking control of the customer conversation*, Penguin Group, New York

Howard, Tamara (2014) *Who's Paying for Lunch?*, Verve Business Books Ltd, Oxfordshire

The sales story   06

Behind every good sale is a great sales story. And it mustn't be fiction. Chapter 5 outlined the classical steps in a sales process and described the key thoughts and feelings experienced by customers at each stage. In addition to this activity, the salesperson must take the potential customer on a 'journey' within each sales meeting. The story they tell is vital to successful consultative selling. It takes a customer on an intellectual and emotional journey, and helps obtain buy-in to what the salesperson is offering.

When does the story begin?

The sales story fits within a company's overall corporate story, which is derived from the overall value proposition, so that it will be consistent and fit seamlessly with the stories sent to the marketplace as a whole, including suspects who have never had any direct contact with the business. So the overall story begins with marketing, and salespeople carry it to potential customers. When the salesperson first becomes engaged with an opportunity at the qualification step, this meeting should be driven by the story itself. The whole interaction should follow an emotional rhythm, with the salesperson driving the process and telling the story.

Why a story?

Telling a story engages the listener on both an emotional and rational level. There is a code, a repeatable pattern to good storytelling. In leadership and in business, stories always follow a similar pattern. Stephen Denning in his books on leadership (Denning, 2007) gives a simple three-step approach to constructing a good story:

1 Get attention through starting with negative stories.

2 Elicit desire through a positive story to get action and buy-in to a vision.

3 Reinforce with reason through using neutral stories to explain what, when, how and why.

Even television commercials follow this pattern within a 30-second or one-minute time frame. Think about headache medication or indigestion tablets. These adverts start by setting the scene and focusing on the problem – a headache or heartburn – perhaps putting the problem into a context with which the target audience can identify. For example, 'Celebrate too much last night and paying the price today? Headache? Queasy?...' The camera focuses on a man, usually with a morning's growth of beard and looking worse for wear, gazing blearily at himself in the mirror.

Next the camera shows him taking the antidote being advertised, with the announcer saying something like, 'To feel better fast, take…!' Then the sequence typically cuts to the same individual in a business suit, looking well-groomed and wide awake, smiling as he engages in a successful business meeting, or in tennis whites, successfully beating his opponent on the tennis court. It doesn't matter which, what matters is that the story has a happy ending. The same process should be used in qualifying sales meetings.

Any sales story begins by setting the scene with a neutral discourse. Next, to engage the listener and maintain interest, the narrative should introduce a change in the emotional intensity. For a sales narrative the easiest and most effective way to introduce this change is to talk about 'what happens if it all goes wrong'. The listener/customer should be led via questioning, down, down, down, until all negative aspects of the current situation have been disclosed, discussed and understood.

Clearly, it is not effective to leave a potential customer depressed and anxious, so a good salesperson should then lead the conversation back up to an emotional 'high'. Typically this shift is accomplished by asking the listener to imagine how good things could be when a problem is solved. If done well, the prospective customer is now in an optimistic state, feeling good and envisioning a positive future with all opportunities exploited and issues addressed. Finally, the meeting ends on a more level, rational basis as the salesperson agrees the next steps.

In psychology, the 'peak-end rule' explains that people judge an experience largely based on how they felt at its peak (ie its most intense point) and at its end, rather than based on the total sum or average of every moment of the experience. The effect occurs regardless of whether the experience is pleasant or unpleasant. Other information aside from that of the 'peak' and the 'end' of the experience is not lost, but it is not used. Listeners absorb net pleasantness or unpleasantness and how long the experience lasted (Fredrickson and Kahneman, 1993). This model says that an event is not judged by the entirety of an experience, but by prototypical moments or snapshots. The remembered value of snapshots dominates the actual value of an experience. Fredrickson and Kahneman theorized that these snapshots are actually the average of the most intense moment of an experience and the feeling experienced at the end. The length of an experience has minimal effect. The peak-end rule is applicable only when an experience has definite beginning and end periods.

In other words, people remember the most intense experiences and the end of the story. If good feelings are stronger than bad, then the overall experience is judged by the good feelings.

This format and pacing mirrors that of all good stories, from children's fairy tales to action thrillers. Enjoyment of the story is as much about experiencing the roller coaster of emotions, as the hero tackles danger after danger and then ends his or her story successfully – 'and they all lived happily ever after...'. Whether or not this rhythm is integral to human nature or, from a young age, almost everyone has been conditioned to expect it – it works. Under all circumstances, it fully engages the listener.

In fact the peak can be at the very beginning if this process is understood and managed well. As writer Darin De Stefano explains, 'The goal of selling something shares a fundamental feature with all human transactions and relationships. In fact, it is a foundational aspect of nature that initial conditions predetermine the scope and form of future outcomes. They also catalyse our felt senses of context and purpose. We are all familiar with the cliché about first impressions; unfortunately, however, we are not technically aware of the power of initial conditions – by which I mean the first moments of contact – to define things like context, role, value, potential and form. The very first impressions, the first gestures and words, the emotional angles of approach – all these features 'initialize' the entire field of play for both parties. All future transactions, successes and failures will naturally inherit not merely character but form from the first few moments of contact.

A deeper knowledge of 'first contact' forms and relations is absolutely crucial to far more than 'controlling the sale' or manipulating a consumer – it is the actual conception-moment of a relationship.

Strong, up-front ground rules

Preparation for this first meeting is critical. It is also important during that 'first contact' and subsequent meetings to manage the psychological 'holding' of the meeting. The salesperson must 'hold the space' and create strong up-front ground rules. This creates a feeling of safety for the customer and aids a more relaxed meeting. Strong up-front ground rules give the following:

- Establishes the content and agenda for the meeting.
- The opportunity for both the salesperson and customer to ask questions.
- Provides each sales meeting with an end result.
- The opportunity for both the customer and the salesperson to say 'no' if there isn't a fit.
- The customer to say 'yes' if there is a good fit.
- Allows for enough time.
- Allows for a decision to be made at each interim meeting.
- Ensures no interruptions.
- Allows participants to deal with their biggest fears up-front. For example, a salesperson who has a fear of asking for money might say, 'Before I begin talking about my company and our expertise, let me tell you my concern. My concern is that we get to the end,

you like what you hear – and I'm going to have difficulty discussing money. So that I can give your problem my full attention, are you okay discussing money up-front?' This conversation must be truthful and not contrived. Only raise concerns if genuinely worried about them. By voicing them up-front it removes their power to overwhelm the salesperson throughout and at the end of the meeting.

Elements of ground rules to include are:

- Appreciation for the meeting.
- Agree a start and end time for the meeting and ensure that this is adhered to.
- State and recap the customer's agenda.
- State and recap the sales agenda.
- State possible outcomes from the meeting, for example: 'One of two things will result from our meeting today. We may see that there is not a fit for our organizations and if that is the case would you be comfortable saying so? On the other hand, we may find a perfect fit and we can then discuss things like budgets and your decision-making process. Would you be comfortable with that?'
- Wrap up and conclude the meeting with very clear next steps.

This emotional journey works very well with any qualifying sales meeting, but is crucial in the consultative sales qualification process.

How? What 'story' is told?

As Dave Gray, founder of XPLANE, the design-thinking consultancy, says:

The creation of selling stories in a workshop environment is heavily dependent upon the expertise of the people in the room with us. There will be blind spots in the current story so we want to get a diverse set of perspectives. Ideally we will get a customer in the room, a salesperson who has spent a lot of time with customers, a person who is technical and able to represent what the product can and cannot do, and someone who represents finance or the executive team. The idea is to get a wide range of perspectives to create a selling story that puts the customer in the centre. We use an 'empathy map' to keep all the different perspectives always customer-focused.

For good transactional selling, marketing or product management will prepare a 'story' that positions a company's product or service as 'the hero'. This story is then integrated into well-prepared sales material and taught to sales staff at each launch. In this way, the salesperson understands why all the thought, engineering and good practice has been put into the new offering to solve customers' problems. The commercial for headache or hangover medicine discussed above is a very simple example of such a targeted story. It focuses on the well-defined group in the market for whom the antidote was developed.

This approach works just as well in the B2B space, but B2B selling is not usually carried out successfully via advertisements. Salespeople become the communicators of the prepared story. That is why, for transactional selling, it is so important for a business to understand and focus on the person who will hear the story – the person who will buy something from them.

Matt Dixon says:

> We wrote about the Grainger example in *The Challenger Sale*. That is rooted in the idea that we've really got to understand at a very deep level what is going on with the customer. We have to figure out what the real pain points are, both rational and emotional, and then figure out what is it that we can offer that ties directly to that. And Grainger did that. It was like the floodgates opened because they were appealing at a very deep, personal and very emotional level to something they do that customers cared about a lot. The way they sell is not by starting with a discussion of Grainger and its history and its products and its services and its mission and values and how many locations they have, and all these kinds of things. They start with a story about the customer and what's going on in the customer's world and that they have a hypothesis. This means the story leads to a very rich discussion with the potential customer. Only then do they lead to the area that Grainger is uniquely qualified in to help the customer address some of their issues. It's a much more powerful way to sell – beginning with the customer and focusing on what's going on in their world and then leading to what makes you unique as a supplier.

Most companies get this horribly wrong by leading with what makes them unique and at that point the customer has really tuned out because they don't really care about that, all they care about is solving their problems and dealing with things going on in their environment.

For transactional selling, a very skilled salesperson can create the story if the company they work for fails to do so, but it is far more effective if the rest of the business's messaging supports the story.

However, consultative selling is different. The selling company's story must support this selling process because designing and implementing the solution will take the co-operation of the whole business. A salesperson alone cannot follow through on any promises made. So, before attempting to sell, the company and the salesperson should work out exactly what it is that the prospective customer is likely to need and then test this solution during the qualification process.

So how does a story fit in to this?

Remember, consultative selling begins with focusing on a prospective customer's business issues and opportunities. The initial qualifying meeting should open on a neutral emotional level with introductions, objectives of the meeting – all neutral topics and all traditional introductions to such a meeting. Rationally, information is exchanged, objectives set out and the scene is set (see Table 6.1).

Next, using directed questioning techniques, the salesperson should probe the customer's attitude and concerns, asking what would happen if nothing is done. He or she should always encourage the customer to contribute quantitative assessments. So, for example, the salesperson might sum up a comment and say, 'So you told me that if your computer system is not complete by 1 January, you will not be able to conduct business. I'm sure you have some sense of what that is worth. How much business would you lose per day? Per month? Of course, there is also the value of loss of customer goodwill.' This quantification of the customer's issues can be used later in the meeting to test price sensitivity and ultimately contribute information for value-based pricing.

After extracting all the information and possible scenarios from the prospective customer, the next step is to 'sum up': 'So you have told me that your company must do something. In our discussion today we have only touched on a few of your key issues and already you have mentioned losses of X/month for every month this situation is

Table 6.1 The emotional journey in the sales meeting

Rational Discussion	Emotional Context
1 Introduction, and clarifying objectives	Neutral
2 Confirm issues/opportunities	Neutral → negative
3 Ask 'what happens if these issues are not addressed or opportunities are not capitalized upon?'	Negative
4 Keep probing for more issues and their impact and try to get detailed answers	Negative
5 Summarize what the customer has revealed	Bottom of the negative state
6 Present optimal solution	Upward movement to more positive mood
7 Check – through questioning – whether optimal solution is practical and get customer to imagine the business to create a positive vision of the desired future	Top of positive peak

not resolved… [the summing up can also include potential gains from an opportunity that needs exploiting]. Clearly it is not appropriate to do nothing; in fact, you need to do something as soon as possible – your business is losing money as we speak. What are you planning on doing? How will you decide? Who else needs to be involved?' For purposes of explanation, these questions are less subtle than a salesperson would phrase them, but the point is clear. By getting to this point in the discussion, not only will the salesperson extract valuable information to be used in pricing and selling, at the same time he/she will also be carrying out the usual qualification necessary at this stage of the sales cycle.

By the time the customer is at the bottom of the emotional dip in this process, the salesperson should be able to determine or confirm:

- that the customer knows there is a problem and that he/she is the person who feels the pain;
- that he/she knows, to some extent, the cost/value of that problem to the business;

- who else is concerned and needs to be involved in selecting a solution;
- the cost of delaying a decision or doing nothing;
- who makes the final decision.

At this stage, the meeting is only half over. The salesperson sums up an understanding of the customer's current business and then says: 'If I could show you a way to... would you be interested in exploring it further?' With this summation and question, he paints a picture of a viable solution and tests whether the customer will or can actually buy anything. In doing so, the mood of the entire meeting shifts to be more optimistic, as possibilities for success are discussed. Remember, this is the first meeting about these issues, there has been no other qualification or RFP or proposal. In fact, a good salesperson will have already shaped the idea of the solution in the mind of the prospective customer. With this question he or she is actually asking for permission to sell. If the customer says, 'Yes, if your company could do that I would be interested', the salesperson can then ask what needs to happen to convince the customer and anyone else in the company.

Should the prospect say no, the salesperson can ask more questions to uncover the objections. Sometimes these will be things that can be overcome and the question is then repeated, 'So, if we overcome X, Y and Z..., then can we explore a solution together?' But sometimes these objections cannot be addressed – after all, this meeting is a qualifying discussion and sometimes prospects qualify-out. The earlier this decision is taken in the sales process, the less time, money and effort is wasted pursuing an opportunity that could never have been won. However, if the prospective customer says yes, then the meeting concludes with plans of the next steps. During the factual and cordial exchange of next steps, the mood returns to a more neutral level as the minds of both the salesperson and the prospective customer focus on future activities and plans. If not already uncovered, at this stage the salesperson should ask:

- What is the company process for making a decision to buy and are there any dates (eg board meetings) that need to be taken into consideration?
- Who else needs to be involved?

- Who makes the final decision?
- Does it have to go to the board?
- Is there a budgeting process or period that needs to be considered?
- Are there specific 'sign off' levels that need to be considered?
- Will the prospect facilitate the internal introductions?
- Timescales... when can decisions be made?

So, if all goes well, the salesperson leaves with a qualified opportunity plus an agreed plan to sell a solution to the rest of the business. The prospective customer remembers the rational discussions and the feelings from the high point and at the end of the meeting – that is, optimistic good feelings plus the neutral feelings around matter-of-fact planning. Lurking in the background is that 'they all lived happily ever after...' feeling that ends a good story.

It all sounds easy – and it can be. An opportunity can go from 0 to 100 miles an hour within an hour-long meeting. However, for the discussion to end successfully there is an enormous amount of planning that happens before the meeting. Remember, this approach is for consultative selling and this means that the salesperson has to have some idea of the combination of products and services that might provide this tailored solution. They must also be certain that their company will support the sale, and this commitment should be obtained before the qualification sales meeting. All these details should be agreed with the salesperson's own company before meeting with the prospective customer. The whole process is, perhaps, best illustrated by an example.

IT services company ABC Ltd had been selling commodity products in the form of 'specialist bodies' to do business and IT consulting, programming, technical design and project management. The business's marketing and service offerings had achieved some level of sophistication, moving from pure Components to Offers. In this capacity it sold implementation services for third-party software and support services, for example: help desk and application support, and systems outsourcing. Yet all these aggregated offerings failed to bridge The Solution Gap between the bottom and the top of the Value Pyramid™ (see Figure 3.5 in Chapter 3). ABC Ltd remained a transactional sales business with a focus on low-cost pricing.

Executive management believed that the company was missing a trick. They put in place a team to configure solutions and design a consultative selling process to support such an approach. Note – the company approached this shift from the top down rather than assigning this task to sales alone. ABC Ltd understood the 1st Law of Selling your Value Proposition: the whole company plays a role in supporting the sales process. This team then looked at the marketplace to understand where there were organizations with the following attributes:

- a market segment with a well-known business issue;
- an issue for which ABC Ltd could configure a solution that pulled together the bulk of its individual capabilities;
- time constraints on the target companies that would induce them to take action sooner rather than later.

The last attribute is important, but not essential. The difficulty in trying to sell solutions to many large corporations is that these organizations have enough money and momentum behind them to sustain significant losses before they need to take action. In many cases, decisions are deferred for as long as possible. Therefore, targeting businesses with a definite, well understood time limit is the most effective way to ensure a decision is taken quickly. Although not used for this example, all the Y2K (Year 2000) computer services illustrate an excellent example of a deadline for taking action. All software amendments had to be completed before the end of the millennium in order to be certain that the business systems would not fail on 1 January 2000. Businesses had no choice, they could not procrastinate – they were forced to fix their systems.

There are additional situations that help focus timely decisions. Some good examples include:

- compliance with government legislation;
- a pending merger or acquisition;
- launch of a new product or service.

All or any of these circumstances can give a decision-making process a sense of urgency that helps to drive the sales process.

Returning to the example of ABC Ltd, it turns out that in one of their target segments there had been a recent change in the law, which meant that all companies in that segment were forced to provide potential customers with specific information before they signed a deal. For most companies in this segment, the computer systems were unable to cope with this legislative demand and, unfortunately, when the law was due to come into effect (about eight months in the future), these businesses would be unable to accept any new business until they could provide their customers with this data. Failure to comply with the law would be very costly.

So, having identified a segment with both a large problem and a time constraint, the working group at ABC Company put together what they believed to be a perfect solution, involving ABC Ltd's products and services, to test a new sales approach for prospective customers in this situation. After designing this solution, the group assembled some sales collateral and began to design a sales approach. In doing so, the team asked a number of questions:

- What companies should they target?
- Who, that is, what role(s) within the company, would feel the most pain in terms of non-compliance?
- How should the salesperson handle the qualifying sales meeting?
- Where had they done something similar to offer 'proof' that ABC Ltd could do what the salesperson claimed?

The simple answer to the last question was 'nowhere' – not in the form of a total solution. However, ABC Ltd as a company had sold and implemented all the separate pieces of the solution many times, so it was simply a matter of configuring proof statements for different parts of the solution. These included: specialist business consulting and business process redesign; outsourcing of the current hardware, software and help desk facilities; and building a new piece of software that coped with the new legislative requirements. In describing the 'how', ABC Ltd decided that the better approach would be essentially to take over the running of all IT services, and it looked at any business processes that could be improved, while setting up and designing new systems that could cope with the new legislation. But the new sales approach didn't focus on the 'how' it focused on the 'what' and the 'so what'. As far the prospective customer was concerned, ABC Ltd was solving a big problem.

The next step was to decide 'who' within ABC Ltd should test this approach on a real opportunity. How would a qualifying meeting proceed and who drove the process? In fact, in this instance, a specialist business consultant was deployed who understood the issues and workings of that business sector. He arranged a meeting with the financial director/operations director and prepared his sales story. After introductions, the consultant asked if the business had plans to address the new legislation – he mentioned one or two other businesses in the same sector who he knew were mustering resources to tackle the issue. The prospect replied that his IT department was 'looking into it'.

'Do you feel confident that your company will meet the deadline?' the consultant asked. *'Even those businesses I work with who already have a programme in place to fix it are a bit concerned.'*

The prospect replied that, no, he did not feel confident.

'What will it cost you if you don't make the deadline?' the consultant probed. *'Have you estimated how much business you might lose?'*

The prospect quoted a big number, something like 2,000 deals per day.

'And what's the average value of a deal?' asked the consultant.

'Oh, they aren't big. Our target market is your working man who pays weekly so it is maybe £100 per day', replied the prospect. *'But we are also worried that this "gap" might give our competitors a chance to move in and that we will lose customers. To date, we have a long history of loyal customers.'*

'Have you estimated those losses? And do you know what it will cost you to try to recapture these lost customers?'

This conversation continued, with the consultant collecting numbers and negative impacts until he exhausted all avenues of exploration. By this time, he had reached the bottom of the emotional dip in his 'sales story'. His next step was to begin to move up the emotional curve to discuss positive outcomes, but first he must ensure that the emotional curve has hit rock bottom and that he has captured and quantified as much as possible, all the negative outcomes. At this point, he sums up and says: *'So, you are telling me that for every day you are late in having a compliant system, you estimate your business will lose £200,000 per day in revenue. Furthermore, you forecast a loss of 2 per cent of your current client base per month* [50,000 is the current client base] *as their policies come up for renewal – and this loss represents approximately £10,000 more per month in future revenues...'* There were additional losses that the consultant summed up. He then went on to suggest, *'So, after one month you are losing at least £6 million, not to mention all the other losses we discuss. Is that right?'*

When the prospect agreed, the consultant then said, *'Well, I don't know for certain if I can help you. I do know we have done something similar for* [he mentions a client reference prepared in advance] *and they saw benefits of X, Y and Z, but we don't know enough about your business or your IT set-up to confirm we can do something similar for you. However, we do have a process that might help. If I could show you a way to move forward and solve your problem in time to comply with the legislation, would you be interested in exploring it with us* [ABC Ltd]*?'*

Of course the prospect said 'yes' and so the consultant continued, the story now moving up the emotional curve to a more optimistic frame of mind.

'We have a process – it takes six weeks', explained the consultant. *'In this process we send in a group of experts who will look at your system and your business processes. At the end of these six weeks, we will not only tell you what it will take to achieve your business objectives, we will provide you with a plan to do it. You then have the choice: either you can do it yourself with your in-house staff, or you can spend a few weeks and write a tender and send it out as a competitive bid, or you can ask us to do the work. The option will be yours.'*

With this offer, the consultant has now shown the prospect a way to solve his problem; the mood is optimistic and things progressed quickly.

'How much will it cost and when can you start?' the prospect asked. And as details of a contract and the next steps were discussed, the mood of the story returned to baseline neutral emotions, but with that 'happily ever after' feeling that comes with the conclusion of a good story.

And the deal was won. Within 18 months, it led to business worth more than £50 million – five times higher than any single deal ever sold previously by ABC Ltd and yielding a much higher margin. Most importantly, ABC Ltd met and exceeded the customer's expectations, so the customer was delighted.

Lessons learned

It would be wrong to say that all it took was a 45-minute meeting for ABC (in the above example) to sell business worth £50 million, although, on the face of it, that's true. Actually, it took weeks of planning and preparation before the meeting in order to make sure it went successfully. In this case, the salesperson was a business consultant; however not all business consultants are capable of driving this sort of sale. In general, the style of selling consulting is very different. In fact in this instance, this individual was chosen for his ability to adapt and change styles and sell in a new way. All his references, the shape of the solution, guideline pricing – particularly for the first phase in which the solution was scoped – had to be agreed with senior management before undertaking the first prospect meeting. And finally, a scoping process needed to be designed that would not only produce a programme that ABC Ltd wanted to deliver but also provided the output that 'sold' the next phase of the programme.

Apart from the need for preparation and the support of the rest of the business, this example illustrates many salient points. The consultant had gained access to a high-level business person, the financial director/operations director. Typically, time is one of the most precious commodities that these individuals possess. A salesperson should never waste the time of such an individual by having nothing to offer in return for their time. That is why, as part of the preparation, the salesperson should always have a 'Plan B', even a 'Plan C', should the prospect not respond as expected. If this individual feels that his/her time has been wasted, then that salesperson will never get a second chance. Always have something to offer that has made the meeting worthwhile.

A second lesson that this example illustrates is the benefit of having a small first step – such as a scoping study – in the process of selling a big solution. Senior executives often have a large discretionary spend or can authorize a reasonable amount without going through a full-blown procurement process. If one can estimate how much this value is – in the example above it was £50,000 – then the first step (ie the first offering sold) should be priced accordingly. Don't worry about profit at this stage; think of this first step as a sales process, so, essentially, the scoping study was paid-for sales effort even though the output was of value to the customer. Also, by contracting with a prospective customer for even a small amount, it breaks an important psychological barrier – the first deal with a particular company. Agreeing this first, smaller contract lowers the barrier to subsequent sales – even if the value of these later deals are much more expensive, it feels easier to buy because there is already an established business relationship.

Another feature to note is that the salesperson positioned this first scoping as part of a much bigger solution. He gave the prospective customer a feeling of control by offering a place in the process where the customer had choice – and a feeling of control is extremely important when a customer is about to 'bet the business' and take a change with a new supplier or partner. Starting small is important. However, positioning the total solution at the beginning of the whole selling process is crucial to the overall sales story and plants a picture of the overall solution in the customer's mind.

Another point to mention is that this sales meeting focused on the person who owned the problem. Anyone trying to sell to this company and solve this problem would have to identify who this person was and somehow arrange a meeting with this individual. That also meant that if the scoping study was approved, all of this person's precious time would be taken up with ABC Ltd, making it unlikely that this person would take the time to deal with anyone else unless ABC Ltd failed to meet expectations. By designing the scoping study to involve the decision maker, he ensured that person would have neither the time nor the inclination to look elsewhere.

Yet still more value came from this 45-minute qualifying meeting: the information gathered during this first meeting provided the salesperson with lots of quantitative information. These numbers served many purposes. As shown in the example, they provided part of a baseline cost for 'the cost of doing nothing'. It is always important to demonstrate to prospective customers that doing nothing has a cost too – and sometimes *not* making a decision ends up costing a business even more than spending money. This cost helps drive a speedy decision and the quicker a sale can be closed, the higher the probability of its success. Finally, another use for these numbers is to help in determining a price for the solution.

Different sales behaviours

To undertake successful consultative selling, a company must select the right sales style. Knowing what behavioural types of salespeople the business should employ is critical. In fact, the sales process may require a whole team of individuals to be involved. When this is the case, it is absolutely vital to understand different styles, where they are appropriate and what happens when any combination of them are together with the customer and trying to progress a sale. The differences between transactional selling and consultative selling have already been explained; however, there are two other styles of selling that also exist: 'solution sales' and 'expert sales'. A quick review of all four styles is useful along with an explanation of where each is the most appropriate.

Transactional sales

The transactional salesperson typically has a specific set of products and/or services to sell. His/her objective is to qualify any prospect as quickly as possible in order to understand whether that person has a need for these well-defined offerings or whether a need can be 'developed'. A good transactional salesperson typically asks a lot of questions and then, if the prospect seems interested, closes as quickly as possible and then moves on to a new prospect. In those situations when no need is established, the salesperson quickly ends the meeting and moves on, saving time and effort to pursue more lucrative opportunities.

The overall style is very directive, uncovering needs and then matching these needs to the features and benefits of whatever is being sold. Typically, this style of selling does not foster close, long-term relationships. The overriding thought behind this type of sales is: 'I only have this (these) product(s) to sell, so I'll find a way to convince you that you have a reason to buy it.' There is no attempt to disguise the fact that this individual is a salesperson and any prospect will immediately recognize the meeting as a sales situation.

If well-trained, these salespeople can be very cost-effective at selling commodity items and some solutions in appropriate circumstances.

Expert service sales

At the other end of the spectrum, 'expert service' salespeople are generally selling their own expertise. Initially the qualifying conversation with a prospective customer starts by getting the prospect to elaborate on a current issue so that the 'expert' can demonstrate how his/her expertise can help. This sales style is typically used by consultants to sell themselves and is often used by anyone trying to sell a specialist service or team.

The overall style is for the expert to talk about what he/she knows in order to demonstrate expertise. In essence, the expert expounds on a topic, hoping that the prospective customer will latch on to a bit of the discourse and say, 'Yes, that's exactly my problem. Can you help me too?' The approach is less selling and more 'being bought from', with the expert setting out his/her stall during the discussion. Because many consultants use this style, many people confuse the approach with consultative selling, which is a different approach entirely. Do not mix the two styles. In expert service sales, the 'salesperson' cedes control of the process to the prospect, while in consultative selling the salesperson drives the selling process.

Solution sales

This style is closest to the transactional style with, perhaps, a bit more of a long-term relationship in mind. The salesperson uses the directed questioning technique in order to encourage a customer to elaborate on business issues so as to uncover and shape an opportunity around which a solution can be proposed. A 'solution' or 'offering' is not as rigid as the commodities offered by a transactional salesperson and, typically, the solution salesperson has more options and flexibility in shaping a deal. In these situations, the directed questioning is less focused on immediate qualification of the opportunity and more on leading the prospect towards elaborating on business issues.

The overall style is one of enquiry and problem solving but the roles are clearly prospect/customer and sales representative. The customer understands exactly what the company has to sell and might see the solution sales rep as their link into the selling company. These salespeople tend to foster longer-term relationships and stick with customers, selling them additional solutions, products and/or services.

Consultative sales

This style is most appropriate for selling on the top half of the Value Pyramid™. While it is clear to everyone involved which company is selling and which is buying, the relationship between the prospective customer and the consultative salesperson is closer to 'peer-to-peer' rather than buyer to salesperson. Why? Because when done well, the salesperson is very knowledgeable about the issues and opportunities in the business segment being addressed. He/she commands the entire resources of the selling company in putting together the optimum solution for the prospect. This individual should command respect and project gravitas.

Although the consultative salesperson also asks a lot of questions, particularly when taking the customer into the 'dip' in the sales story, this individual also speaks knowledgeably about the marketplace and how other businesses have dealt with some of the issues. So questions tend to combine both features, inserting a referencing statement into the interrogation. An example of such a question is: 'In my experience I have found that…; what about you? Is this true in your business?' A consultative salesperson tells the sales story and uses it to drive a solution sale to a successful close.

So, there are four very different styles that should be applied in four very different situations. Sometimes, when using teams of people to drive a sale, some or all of these styles may be deployed at different stages of the process or when dealing with different people in the 'buyer map'.

Therefore, for large, complex deals it is critical to understand which styles are needed where and when. These individuals will then be mapped off against different people within the prospective customer's organization. In order for all of them to drive forward the sales process to a successful conclusion there should be a clearly articulated set of sales activities with one person (a salesperson with overall accountability for winning the business) in charge and orchestrating the activities. Without such a plan, the result can be disastrous.

What can happen when a company mixes sales styles when pursuing an opportunity?

Imagine a qualifying sales meeting in which a solutions or consultative salesperson brings along an expert salesperson from the same company. Typically, the first two types would drive the meeting by asking questions – usually questions for which they already have some idea of the answer, but the whole point of the process is to get the prospective customer to speak the answer. Then you have the expert salesperson who needs to show what he/she knows. When this person hears a question, he/she answers it – almost without thinking – to illustrate expertise.

Now imagine the frustration and confusion in a sales meeting when the consultative salesperson asks a question and his/her own companion chirps up and answers it before the customer can speak. This meeting would continue with 'question' and 'answer' followed by more 'question' and 'answer' with the prospective customer unable to say anything. Why? Because these two salespeople are following different playbooks.

How frequently does this situation really occur?

The answer is: very often. Especially in a technical sale when a salesperson feels he/she needs the backup of technical expertise. What's missing in this situation is a clear process in which both salespeople understand the roles that each should play in the process. In this instance, during a qualifying meeting, the expert salesperson should remain quiet until and unless called upon to speak by the solution/consultative salesperson. There are instances when expert salespeople can sell 'their expertise' in a complex, solution sale, but it is typically at a later stage in the sales process.

Mixing a transactional sales style with any other is also a disaster. Remember, this salesperson is only interested in qualifying and closing. Any other discussions will be perceived as irrelevant and a waste of time. This salesperson will view the extended discourse of the expert or the storytelling of the consultative salesperson as too much talking. Too much talking by anyone but the prospective customer is counter to everything that a transactional salesperson has been taught. On the other hand, if the transactional salesperson starts the conversation, he/she will try to 'close down' the discussion to focus on 'the deal'; the solutions salesperson will try to 'open up' the conversation to explore possible solutions. The expert salesperson will just be horrified. These specialists are 'bought from' because someone values their expertise, and often they don't even consider themselves as salespeople. As a result, in any meeting with a transactional salesperson, the expert would be embarrassed and horrified at being associated with such strong and crass examples of selling.

And yes, this situation happens too – typically when competing parts of the business send someone from separate sales forces within the business to pursue an opportunity together. Because these siloed divisions are competing against each other rather than against external competitors, the customer ends up confused and annoyed. This situation will not occur in companies that are customer-centric, but it is all too common in large businesses whose view of the world is entirely inwardly focused.

Law 9 of Value Proposition Selling states that, 'You can't mix your selling styles in one meeting, eg consultative with transactional. For team selling scenarios, you must have a team selling process with clearly delineated roles and responsibilities.'

So, what are the attributes of a 'good' salesperson of any style?

Essentially, a good salesperson should be a storyteller. Like all story-tellers, they should be a bit dramatic and instructive and, above all, engaging and entertaining. Although these may not be the traits listed in most selling manuals, the key attributes are:

- entertaining;
- creative;
- engaging;
- intelligent;
- personable;
- challenging.

Some of the skills necessary are similar to those of a teacher. The salesperson should be able to:

- inform;
- teach;
- direct;
- guide;
- – and do so gently without insulting the intelligence of prospective customers.

Of course, in addition, all salespeople should be experts in the products, services, solutions and processes of the business they represent.

Team selling

Mentioned earlier in this chapter, large, complex deals often require a team of people to progress the sale. In the example of 'storytelling' and ABC Ltd, although the scoping study was paid for, it was, in fact, a team selling process that delivered a plan for the customer as well as a proposal for more work. In other instances, proposal preparation can require a team of experts and specialists and this team may include all sales styles. For team selling, a clearly articulated process is required and individuals should be mapped against specific customer roles as appropriate. Each individual should be assigned specific responsibilities and the overall leader of the process should be the consultative salesperson.

To provide a detailed explanation of the process would be the topic of a separate book. Needless to say, the whole process should be managed like a project, with project management disciplines, communications and documentation.

For team selling – in fact, for all solutions selling – what is critical is:

- the right people (or team);
- the right process;
- a common understanding by the whole company of what they want to sell and how it will be delivered;
- a Plan 'B' for the approach to the customer;
- a clear understanding of the prospective customer, his/her business issues/opportunities and what the customer understands and values.

Sales approaches, team processes, sales processes, sales styles and stories – many successful companies employ all these things and do so successfully. But many more companies do not. Some businesses, particularly those that focus on product or expertise, fail to appreciate the skill and complexity involved in the go-to-market process and they ignore it to their detriment. The 10 Laws of Value Proposition Selling provide a good check list for any business wishing to develop an authentic market positioning and selling style and approach.

Self-test: how to improve your listening skills and empathy in sales

Here are a few exercises to practise in order to enhance your behavioural selling and storytelling skills by using empathy and listening:

1 *Imagine yourself as your customer*
   Easy to say, much harder to do. This requires that you practise a shift in perspective. Empathy requires that you feel what your customer is feeling. It is not imagining what they are feeling but rather actually *feeling* what they are feeling. This helps build connection and trust. Practise, practise, practise. When listening to your customer you should

be able to feed back to them, in a way that they resonate with the following:

- Your customer's perception of the points they were sharing with you.
- What was troubling them about what they told you?
- What emotions are being expressed by your customer in this moment?
- What does your customer need from you at this moment? Just to listen and reflect back what they are saying? Or are they in discursive mode? Have they moved into a more rational, problem-solving mode?

2   *Recognize your own emotions and then you will be able to recognize other people's more easily*
Empathy is about the ability to share in another person's emotional experience. You need to pay careful attention to their verbal cues and their body language. How do their words and body language tell you about what they are feeling?

- Ask a family member or friend to observe you as you tell them an emotive story.
- Ask them about the verbal and body language cues they can observe in you. What are they? How do they manifest?

When you understand your own behaviour and emotions better you will find it easier to identify this in others.

3   *Listen and accept what is being told to you*
In sales we spend a lot of time and effort trying to change people's minds. Too often we are in too much of a hurry to do this rather than taking the time to listen, understand and respect the customer's views and opinions. Would you want someone to change your mind without first taking the time to understand what it is you believe and why you believe it?
Practise this with a family member again:

- Ask them to tell you an emotive story about something that happened to them.
- You need to suspend all your judgement and just listen.
- Occasionally paraphrase small parts of what they told you and repeat this back to them.
- Ask them at the end if they felt you were truly listening and were really trying to understand what they were telling you.

4   *Use emotions to drive actions*

As we have seen in this chapter already, there is an emotional journey in telling a good sales story. Good salespeople use negative emotions to create a case for change and drive the customer to take action. They use positive emotions to build hope and a vision for a positive solution to the customer's problems:

- Make a list of questions that uncover the implications for the customer if there is no change.

- Then make a list of questions that elicit a vision of the implications if the change is made.

- Describe what that change would look like.

- How would the customer know that the change had been made?

- What actions would have to be taken to get there?

NOTE The above list has been modified and reproduced with kind permission from Anthony Iannarino (2010).

References

Denning, Stephen (2007) *The Secret Language of Leadership*, Jossey-Bass, San Francisco

Fredrickson, Barbara and Kahneman, Daniel (1993) Duration neglect in retrospective evaluations of affective episodes, *Journal of Personality and Social Psychology*, **65**(1), pp 45–55

Iannarino, Anthony (2010) [accessed 13 January 2017] 5 Ways to Improve Your Empathy and EQ in Sales [Blog] [Online] https://thesalesblog.com/2010/02/28/5-ways-to-improve-your-empathy-and-eq-in-sales/

Winning business

07

The 10 Laws of Value Proposition Selling

Now this story is drawing to a close. As in a sales story, there is a decision to be taken, questions to be answered and next steps to plan. Answer the questions posed in this chapter and you have a choice either to do nothing or to move towards becoming a selling organization. If you take this step and follow the laws of value proposition selling, both your business and your customers will benefit. Before you make this decision, we will review the steps and the laws.

Your first consideration is to be authentic: to truly care about what your customers value in order to focus the whole business on maintaining and building this value. Some businesses have undertaken value proposition work with the objective of papering over the cracks or adding some marketing sparkle so as to appear to embrace what customers value. Customers are not fooled by this – eventually, they will see through the device.

Getting any benefit from value proposition work means transforming many things within the business, including processes, structure and behaviours. Unless a business approaches these efforts in earnest, value proposition work can be a waste of time and money. However, when conscientiously applied, it can create a treasure chest filled with items that customers value.

The techniques described in this book for turning a value proposition into a sales proposition are powerful. They should only be deployed when what is being sold benefits both the customer and the selling company. These techniques are not about marketing spin;

they have been designed to help authentic businesses focus their efforts and sell effectively, not to manipulate customers into buying something they don't need or want. Selecting the best sales approach and style, and crafting the sales story are very effective and proven approaches.

The sales story helps a business to integrate all its functions – often bringing together previously siloed departments within the company. In this way, the whole company understands what the business sells and how every employee can support the sales process. Whether an opportunity is driven by a lone salesperson or a sales team, in reality selling is a team sport, and an outcome to which everyone is working.

Law 1: the whole company plays a role in supporting the sales process

Enough about the selling company – the whole point of value proposition work is to extend the company psyche to include the customer inside a business's ecosystem (most large businesses do not) and make the business more customer-centric. The customer must become an organ within the anatomy of the business body, and not be seen as 'an other' on the outside. No matter the business type, product or service, offering or solution, anything sold should be designed with a target customer type in mind. Who better to question in order to understand these needs than prospects and customers? Great companies take this process further to include suppliers and collaborators too. Appropriate insights from all of these individuals provide valuable information for a business to use in refining its offerings and amending its go-to-market approach.

Businesses need to engage their employees in the selling process too. Those that don't are missing a trick and leaving revenue on the table. Worse than that, disengaged employees can have a negative impact on sales. As we will see in Chapter 8, in companies like Gore and Semco, an inclusive approach makes employees feel more engaged and genuinely part of the business, which can positively affect both their productivity and loyalty. By understanding and delineating the role that each can play, the company gains the chance to improve operational efficiency too. Focusing all the employees on helping the sales process from within their roles is a win–win–win situation for the employees, the business and its customers.

Law 2: the customer is part of the business system

Value proposition work helps businesses to understand what their customers value and, by understanding this value, to structure the company to create a win–win outcome for both. The benefits of genuine customer-centricity are numerous: for example, less customer churn, the ability to price on true value, higher barriers to entry for competitors, and high customer engagement. However, like any relationship, the customer relationship takes work and reflection. The Value Proposition Builder™ is a way to periodically assess this relationship, giving a business the opportunity to realign the company to remain customer-centric.

Qualitative interviews, analysed by specially trained individuals, lead to illuminating insights. In almost all 600-plus examples of value proposition work using the Value Proposition Builder™ process, the participating businesses were surprised (usually pleasantly and occasionally unpleasantly) by their customers' responses. Those companies that followed through and implemented organizational changes saw substantial benefits, while those that did not gained far less, sometimes nothing. The businesses that made no changes did not extend their business ecosystem to include their customers, and continued to maintain an 'us' and 'them' attitude and behaviours.

Building on what customers value does *not* mean doing everything they request. The customer is not always right. What it does mean is gaining a clear appreciation of what customers value about doing business with a company, building on these things, where possible, and understanding where adjustment within the selling business can help resolve customer issues or irritations. Value proposition work provides the information on which a business can make informed decisions and plans.

Law 3: the structures and behaviours of a business must be kept in balance with each other

The leading psychologist and founder of transactional analysis, Eric Berne, wrote extensively about organizations. His theory of organizations as being driven by a combination of structures and behaviours (or what he called 'dynamics') provides a thought-provoking challenge to businesses today (Berne, 1963). Structures – including processes, organization charts and tangible ways of structuring the organization – provide the business with support; Dynamics – people's behaviours you see in the business every day – provide the business with energy. Together the structures and behaviours define the culture of the organization. When in balance, the structures and behaviours together create a healthy and supportive culture; when out of balance, where either the structures or the behaviours have the majority power, the culture tends either to be stifling or chaotic.

Where the structures are few or loose then the dynamics-led organization tends to have a culture of being personality-led and responds to the individual(s) with power. Conversely, the structures-led organization, where the dynamics are subservient to the processes, has a culture that feels more authoritarian and stifling.

Those businesses that truly want to become selling organizations and to have an authentic selling culture must define and create clear and balanced structures and dynamics that allow that culture to flourish. Selling culture, therefore, is not an accident but rather is carefully designed, crafted and managed.

But as we have seen already in this book, sales activities are not the only process that will need adjusting – marketing, customer service, finance, even procurement and delivery systems will need examining and adjustment. In fact, all connections between the business and the outside world – suppliers, customers, even the local neighbourhood and wider environment – should come under the microscope. It is vital to balance the whole commercial ecosystem of a business.

Probably the most difficult change to assess and amend is 'attitude' and 'employee behaviours'. Remember Law 1: the whole company sells? To successfully implement this law, all employees must believe it. Leading by example is a good start, with the executive team 'walking the walk'. Don't underestimate staff; employees will spot hypocrisy very quickly, so lead by example and mean it or the company will undergo the wrong sort of behaviour change – where it is okay to say one thing, but do another.

Another factor implicit in change processes and behaviours that are implemented on a company-wide scale is that value proposition work should have visibility, endorsement and sponsorship at the most senior level. In large organizations with traditional structures, these are the only individuals empowered to make these changes. It is virtually impossible to try to change such an organization from the bottom, or even the middle, upward. So for value proposition work, gain executive buy-in or don't bother.

Law 4: sales behaviours must be directed towards helping the customer gain maximum value from sales offerings

In an authentic business, sales staff will only sell where the prospective customer has a genuine need. That said, not every prospective customer clearly understands complex business issues or all the options available to solve them. One of a salesperson's jobs is to guide the customer, helping him or her to understand options, including the option of doing nothing, and educating these individuals about the benefits of selecting a particular option. Ideally, this option is what the salesperson is selling, but that might not always be the case.

In the short term, it may take a bit longer to qualify appropriate opportunities. But in the long term, by carefully selecting customers who will benefit from a company's offering, the salesperson can use all the selling tools and methods available to help the customer buy his/her company's offering. What this approach also demands is that all sales propositions should be designed within the business, drawn from the value proposition from the top down and not from the bottom up.

One example is the common practice of trying to design an offering in order to justify a desired price increase. Many companies take this approach. Someone – the CEO or financial director or shareholders – says that it is about time to get a 2 per cent, 10 per cent or even 20 per cent price rise. That's it: they just want a price rise and leave it to the salespeople to justify the increase to the customer. This common practice can, of course, be implemented and work for a while, but the approach has nothing to do with using a sales proposition that is derived from a value proposition. It is just about doing what the company has always done, selling in the same way, and merely increasing prices.

Driven by a value proposition, this process would happen differently. There could still be a price increase, but the sales proposition would be different, as would the sales approach and sales story. Using this methodology, the business would start with its marketing strategy and determining its desired position on the Value Pyramid™. This would then dictate how the offering would be packaged, including understanding its value to the customer. Pricing would be the final step. There might still be a 2 per cent, 10 per cent, 20 per cent or even larger price rise, but the process would start with the customer, rather than just demanding the desired revenue stream.

Law 5: understand and be clear about the difference between marketing and selling

One reason for the confusion between these two terms is that many companies and individuals who sell are embarrassed to use the 's' word: for them it has many negative connotations. So instead they have developed terms such as 'marketing representative' to describe the role. While sales staff can be viewed as representatives and/or ambassadors of a business's marketing strategy, the sales role is very different. To clarify the difference between the two, a simple definition of marketing is a useful place to start.

In general, marketing focuses on:

- Market: identifying, delineating and quantifying the opportunity (market research).

- Customer type: identifying 'the need' being satisfied and the triggers that would cause customers to buy.

- Offering: packaging the offering, whether product, service or solution, in terms that are attractive to the target customer and market (service offer development and product management). In addition, marketing should feed back information to appropriate departments should any part of the offering no longer be appropriate, so that modifications can be made.

- Demand: marketing can try to influence 'demand' and customer expectations via all communication material (collateral, website, postings/articles, advertising) as appropriate to the product type and industry (market communications).

- Competition: analysing competitive offers, positioning and risk to the business.

- Price: understanding the value to the customer and competitive offerings so as to set the optimal price for sales and profits.

- Sales channels: ideally, marketing should identify and recommend the best channels to market to support the business's profitable growth.

- Internal messaging and communications to the rest of the company's ecosystem.

The Value Pyramid™ helps to position a company's offerings – both current and aspirational – in terms of the value to the target customer. This positioning then dictates the optimal sales approach.

In general, marketing has both a long-term (eg the strategy) and short-term (eg events, advertising) function. In contrast, the sales role is more short term.

Sales, at its most fundamental, is about closing deals and helping to educate prospective and existing customers about the benefits of a particular business's offerings. In most companies, sales goals are short-term aspirations with sales targets set for daily, weekly, monthly or quarterly sales. In some businesses, with very complex deals and bidding structures, the sales targets can even be measured in years. In general, the further down the Value Pyramid™, the faster the sale and the more short term the selling focus. Closing deals, however, can take many forms:

- understanding the customer's problem;
- being bought from, eg retail shops, web-based selling, even sales of expert professionals (marketing plays a huge role here, in creating demand and 'pull');
- identifying customers with appropriate need and closing the sale (transactional sales);
- developing the need and closing (solution selling and consultative selling);
- co-developing the need with the customer and fulfilling this need (consultative selling);
- developing a joint solution (strategic consulting, joint-venture selling).

All of these approaches are supported by marketing initiatives that create demand and market awareness.

Law 6: ensure that all business processes support the market positioning

When a business shifts a level on the Value Pyramid™, everything changes. This book has focused on the changes in sales approach and some of the necessary adjustments in marketing. However, all of the business must adapt, from customer service to delivery, from production to procurement. Imagine shifting from commodity to high-value services and not making the necessary adjustments to customer service and delivery. All the company's action must support the sales proposition.

Imagine buying a Tiffany's diamond bracelet and having it handed to you in a cheap plastic bag with no wrapping or protection. Imagine selling such an item at a discount store or superstore and still trying to obtain the same premium pricing. Imagine buying this jewellery – at full price – from a website that delivers it in cheap packaging in the regular post? In all these instances, the delivery does not support the market image and pricing of the product. In these retail scenarios the disconnect is obvious. But in some B2B environments the situation is less apparent and the same anomalies occur.

A common example is when customers sign up for large, even multimillion-pound, highly profitable contracts and then cannot reach a real person in the business when problems arise. Or customers who pay a premium for extra service and then the contracting company fails to provide it at all touch points. A contract is a promise and businesses should be organized to fulfil those promises or, ultimately, revenues will suffer.

Law 7: don't try to change everything all at once; you need an evolutionary plan

Gene Leonard, Managing Director of LBS Partners, a leading Lean transformation consultancy, made the following observation when it came to deciding to change his organization:

> The content in the research interviews was absolutely key for us. The feedback, what clients said about our business, was quite different from what we would have thought they would say. It was more positive and more complimentary than we had imagined. The words that came out were quite humbling for us – that we were very trusted by our clients – and that has had a huge impact both in our confidence and the way we go to market. However, the clients also said they wanted our business to take on a wider role beyond the niche operational space we had been working in. As a result of the richness of the research process, we felt able to change the organization significantly – but we did it gradually over a two-year period. We had to innovate. It was difficult and it was essential. Over those two years we rebuilt our organization.

Changing processes and behaviours in a large organization is not a one-step process. It requires a programme plan, commitment at the most senior levels and resources to implement the plan. However, the end result is well worth the effort. Like all change programmes, some best practice should be followed:

- Understand and honestly assess the existing processes.
- Create, articulate and communicate a vision of the desired, transformed business.
- Design an evolutionary programme that enables the company to carry on doing business while implementing the changes.
- Put in place appropriate milestones and measures to ensure that business is making progress.
- Communicate, communicate, communicate. Let employees, customers and anyone else in the company ecosystem know what is happening. Communicate progress and success in a manner appropriate to each audience.

In making these changes, particularly behaviour changes, there are some cornerstones for success:

- Lead from the top and demonstrate the behaviour changes that are needed.
- Reward or recognize the right behaviours.
- Make the shift an evolutionary process, especially for existing customers who will be suspicious of sudden changes in approach, style or offerings.
- Create a credible sales story that incorporates the old way with the new approach.

Now let's focus on the sales proposition as a special example of these changes. Assume that a business has been selling at the Components level of the Value Pyramid™. Existing customers will expect a transactional selling style based on price, service and/or delivery times. The existing salesperson will have a good relationship with most of his/ her customers who will be used to this style and approach. Now, after value proposition work, the company decides that it never intended to be a commodity supplier and that this placement was 'accidental' – driven by the market rather than the company's market strategy. The executives involved in the work determine that their business, in fact, can and should sell Solutions.

This situation poses a challenge. Changing a transactional selling style to a consultative style is very difficult and is often an impossible shift for some sales professionals to make. In addition, these customers who are buying on a transactional basis have been providing the bulk of the business revenues. So, how does the business make this shift without endangering its revenue stream and annoying its customers? How can the existing transactional salesperson help in this situation?

The answer is: slowly and carefully. When asking a salesperson to alter the selling style with existing customers, it forces both salesperson and customer out of their respective comfort zones. So to make this change, merely mouthing words is not enough – people 'leak' emotions when they are nervous or uncomfortable, both in their choice of words and body language. Therefore, lots of preparation and coaching of the sales staff may be required so that they feel comfortable and confident with the new approach. The salesperson should be made to feel upbeat and comfortable with any new offering and he/she will now offer something even better to the customer. These positive feelings put the customer at ease and make credible whatever message is delivered.

So, how might such a sales meeting take place? If, typically, the salesperson leads with a product specification and/or a price list, leave some of this process in place, but add to it. That way both the salesperson and the customer have familiar territory upon which to start discussions. Then, let the salesperson introduce a new solution as well.

He/she can say, 'In addition to our usual products/services, we have been looking at your needs and market trends and have spent the last few years developing something that will address them. We can now offer you "X" [whatever solution is relevant] at a price of "Y". If you find it useful, wonderful, if not, we still offer all of the usual products/services you have been buying – this new solution is just something extra.'

Then, over time, the company can either add to this solution or create more new solutions until such a time as a greater part of its offerings are now solutions. In this way, some of the existing sales staff can make the transition to a different style, while some customers – they won't all do it – shift their buying from commodity to solutions. The key is to make the shift evolutionary, not revolutionary.

While this explanation makes the whole process sound easy – it isn't. There is a huge psychological barrier that those individuals who interact with existing customers must be helped to cross. Selling is a challenging job and harder still when an experienced salesperson is asked to alter an approach or style. Coaching may help as well as carefully prepared scripts or role-plays to provide him/her with the confidence to attempt a new skill.

Law 8: use the sales process as a guide and select the appropriate sales approach and style for your market positioning

Many businesses, particularly technical or engineering businesses, lump all things 'sales' into one big category. To fully exploit the tools and techniques presented in earlier chapters, it is crucial to understand the differences between:

- Sales process: the stages are the same for all, but the techniques for moving through the process are different depending on what is being sold and the sales approach.
- Sales approach: transactional or consultative.
- Selling style: transactional, expert, solutions or consultative.

For any given marketing strategy, companies should select the most appropriate sales approach and style for their business. Mixing styles can be disastrous.

The sales process lists the stages of any sales opportunity – starting from suspect through to contracting the deal; whether or not a company uses a documented sales process, *all sales* follow these stages. For some types of selling it can all happen quickly, even in one meeting; for others, the process can take months or years. Deploying a documented sales process is a useful way to:

- manage sales;
- forecast sales;
- inform others in the business what is happening with any given opportunity;
- map sales support needs.

The sales process exists regardless of the industry involved, the sales approach selected or the selling style. It is universal.

The sales approach relates to how a company's offerings are positioned in the marketplace. Transactional selling supports efforts on the lower half of the Value Pyramid™ and consultative selling, the upper two layers. The two types of selling are very different and, typically, a different sales force is used for each:

- Use transactional selling for commodity or amalgamated offerings.
- Use consultative selling for solutions or joint ventures.

The sales style

There are, fundamentally, four different sales styles and each is appropriate for different situations:

- transactional;
- expert;
- solution;
- consultative.

Do not confuse the consultative selling style with 'selling consulting' – the two are very different and selling consulting is closer to the expert style of selling.

Sales skills

All discussions in this book have assumed that all or any salesperson will possess competent, core selling skills. These skills have not been covered, not because they are not vital, but because there are literally hundreds of authors who have written about the topic already. So, while one cannot make a good meal without high-quality ingredients, it is also impossible to create a high-performing sales force if they do not possess the basic skills.

Law 9: you can't mix your selling styles in one meeting

You must have a team selling process with clearly delineated roles and responsibilities – you cannot mix your selling styles (eg consultative with transactional) in one meeting. This mixing of different representatives and styles from the same selling business is such a common but significant error that it merits its own separate law. How can a business determine whether it regularly makes this mistake? A business that uses a well-defined sales process and approach will find itself in this position less often. Selling is not 'one size fits all'. Companies should invest the time and effort in understanding what is most appropriate for their particular business. Given these basics, there are some rules that can be followed to avoid the perils of accidentally and inappropriately mixing sales types in one meeting:

- Never send two or three different (and competing) sales types to a qualifying meeting 'just in case'.

- Always prepare, do research and then make a judgement about which sales type would be more appropriate. Hedging bets and sending them all will most likely end in a lost opportunity and an annoyed or confused prospective customer.

- Never send inappropriately skilled sales staff to customer meetings, particularly the qualifying meetings.

- Always make it clear who is in charge when there are two or more representatives from your company in a sales meeting. Whoever is in charge has final accountability for making a successful sale and should direct the conversation.

Law 10: this process – the value proposition work and organizational adjustments – never stops

If there is one fundamental principle in business, it is that everything changes: the market, customers and their requirements, suppliers, employees, government legislation... the list goes on. The Value Proposition Builder™ process is an excellent way to help manage change and design for future innovation.

Once a company has carried out value proposition work, it should have developed the skills and behaviours to continuously assess its business 'treasures' and understand the entire business ecosystem. Coaching may help in driving forward the process and guiding appropriate behaviours but, fundamentally, such a company will have shifted to a more customer-centric business and the necessary adjustments will become easier and easier to implement without external help. This condition will leave a company in a far healthier position to respond to customers and the market, and to deliver profitable business.

By following these laws you have the foundation you need to start building a selling organization: one that is customer-centric, resilient and responsive to change.

Reference

Berne, Eric (1963) *The Structures and Dynamics of Organizations and Groups*, Grove Press, New York

Creating
the selling
organization

08

We started this book with a contemporary paradox. Although customers have more power than ever, they are less satisfied with the businesses that serve them. As we have seen, this customer power comes from factors like ubiquitous technology, easy access to information, growing competition and the spread of globalization.

And as this book has illustrated so far, many businesses are failing to meet expectations. They are not putting the customer first (even though many are likely to say that they do) and not building their sales propositions on the things that customers genuinely value. As a result, they are missing opportunities and getting attacked by disruptive competitors.

We have examined how to tackle this problem head-on – first by developing a value proposition that is rooted in a genuine understanding of customers, and then translating it into powerful customer sales propositions. Then we looked at how best to deploy appropriate sales approaches at the right time, backed up by sales stories that take customers on an emotional journey.

Throughout the book we've featured organizations that have put this new approach into practice to different degrees, in every case with a measure of success. In fact for some of the organizations featured, it has transformed the way they work.

The subtitle of this book is 'How to transform your business into a selling organization'. If, like the businesses we've featured, you follow the approach outlined so far, there is much to be gained. Organizations have created entirely new, successful business lines, stemmed losses and reconnected with customers they had been losing. It is powerful stuff.

But the most success has come from when people create a 'selling organization'. This does not just refer to an efficient sales operation (although sales should definitely be efficient). Much more than 'papering over the cracks' – rebranding, for example – it is about transforming into the type of organization that is totally focused on meeting customer needs. A key component of this is to achieve the right balance between organizational structures and behaviours.

> 3rd Law of Value Proposition Selling: the structures and behaviours of a business must be kept in balance with each other.

If structures are more dominant the organization will be too rigid and inflexible; however, if behaviours dominate then the organization will tend to have a culture of being personality-led and responding to the individual(s) with power.

Sounds easy, right? Indeed for some organizations, it is. If you are a start-up, without a sprawling, legacy structure to deal with, it is not hard to build everything you do around the customer. Many of the disruptors in financial services – such as Metro Bank, which uses internal social networks to spur innovation – are doing this. Even larger organizations, and even those in the public sector, can make the change too. As Aylesbury Vale District Council (featured in Chapter 2) shows us, a local authority can be an agile innovator with the right customer insights, leadership and motivation.

For many businesses, though, the path to becoming a selling organization is harder. The key reason is that this kind of organization is very different from the traditional hierarchical structures that have prevailed for so long.

A 'selling organization' has more in common with a biological system. It is flexible, and open to new ideas and influences. It learns fast from its experiences and its errors. It includes plenty of strong feedback loops. And it is prepared to take risks and to trust its partners.

Describing this as 'redesigning for resilience', business thinker Giles Hutchins illustrates the idea simply.

All organizations are somewhere on a spectrum between these two extremes – although the old-fashioned hierarchy on the left-hand side of Figure 8.1 is still very persistent today.

Figure 8.1 Hierarchy versus resilient design

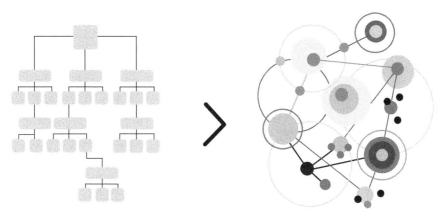

SOURCE Hutchins, 2016a

It does not take an imaginative leap to instantly see how difficult it can be to make quick, responsive decisions in a traditional organization. An issue is referred up through layers of management, where it can get stuck in silos, overlaid with the assumptions of senior managers, and generally lost. And if there are multiple P&Ls held by different people in the different silos, this causes problems too: a new solution that cuts across business lines might be profitable in one country, but loss-making in another. Anyone who has worked in an organization of any scale is likely to have experienced one or more of these difficulties.

The old style of organization has its roots in the Industrial Revolution and the principles of 'scientific management', when a business was entirely focused on making products as efficiently as possible and then 'pushing' them out to the market. Hutchins (2016b; see also 2016c) describes this as the 'machine paradigm':

The responsibility for optimizing the organizational *machine* became management's domain and their primary concern. This mechanistic logic coupled with economies of scale, centralization and control-based thinking led to the hierarchical organization structure with its silos and bureaucracy we know only too well today. Employees were relegated to the role of efficiently performing the duties as defined by management. As management seeks to improve the efficiency of the machine, they unwittingly undermine the creativity, agility and empowerment of people in the process... No matter how we try to reconfigure a machine, the very idea of a machine means it is not very agile or creative and, notwithstanding our love of technology, we rarely feel passion for, or commitment to the machine.

Hutchins summarizes the differences between a 'machine' and 'living' organization as follows:

Table 8.1   Differences between mechanistic and living organizations

Machine	The Living Organization
Produces	Creates
System of discrete components	Organic interdependent relationships
Does as it is told	Learns and adopts
Purpose is to 'do'	Purpose is to serve
Predict and control	Sense and respond
Transactional	Relational

SOURCE Hutchins, 2016b

Ways to create the selling organization

How do you build a selling organization? There is no single, tried-and-tested method. Business has been experimenting with alternative ways of organizing itself for many years. What has emerged is a range of approaches, all of which have been successful in different ways and to different degrees. For some organizations these have been the foundation for stellar growth or decades-long success; for others, they have been experiments that worked until the old ways took hold again.

Small, semi-autonomous teams

Even the corporate monolith General Motors (GM), which ground to a halt in 2009 and had to be bailed out by the US government, had successes in its history when it organized along more 'natural' principles. Company president Alfred P Sloan introduced a system where autonomous business units were co-ordinated centrally. According to

Karl Ludvigsen (2009), this created 'a vibrant enterprise whose operating divisions were close to their markets and individually creative. They also commanded great brand loyalty. GM's divisions fought harder with each other than they did with their external rivals, creating a competitiveness that generated fine products and appreciative customers.'

Because full-scale transformation is such a massive challenge, organizations often use spinoffs or small specialist divisions to experiment with new approaches. The term 'skunkworks' originates from defence contractor Lockheed Martin, which set up the eponymous division that ultimately created some of its most celebrated innovations. In the book *Leading Innovation, Creativity and Enterprise* (Cook, 2016) the author Peter Cook explains why size is important when it comes to innovating in a business context. He cites 'Dunbar's number', which, at 150, is the maximum size of a hunter-gatherer community and the 'cognitive limit' on the number of people with whom it is possible to have stable relationships.

The experience of GM shows how it is possible to create a 'selling organization' – in fact, several of them – within a large company. Its success in its glory years can be attributed at least in part to the fact that small, autonomous divisions could be much more responsive, with teams closer to one another and to customers. As a result, they were able to develop clear sales propositions that resonated emotionally with customers. Once the company consolidated and centralized, it lost this advantage. The rest is history.

Decentralized organizations

Visa International

Visa International was developed in the 1960s on entirely decentralized principles. Founder Dee Hock created a highly collaborative organization designed to deal with its complex marketplace, where its bank customers had simultaneously to co-operate and compete with one another. Hock has variously described Visa as 'largely self-organizing', 'enabling' and 'management-proof'. Indeed when Hock left Visa to go farming for a few years, the company carried on its successful trajectory (Waldrop, 1996).

History suggests that Hock's 'whole organization' approach has been more resilient than autonomous teams at GM. According to Ludvigsen, the automaker's failure came about as it gradually lost touch with its customers. Visa remains a multibillion-dollar global organization that has not needed bailouts to build and maintain its strong market position.

WL GORE & Associates

Materials manufacturer WL Gore & Associates describes its structure as a 'flat lattice'. It is designed to encourage individual initiative from its employees, who are called 'associates'. In sharp contrast to the traditional corporate hierarchy that co-founder Bill Gore had experienced at chemical company Du Pont, the company has 'no traditional organizational charts, no chains of command, nor predetermined channels of communication'.

Associates don't have bosses, but are instead accountable to fellow team members. And rather than being forced into specializations, they are encouraged by 'sponsors' to find projects that match their ability and skills. According to Gore, leaders are more likely to emerge naturally than to be appointed, and they are defined by 'followership'.

Four guiding principles for all associates hold the lattice together:

- fairness to each other and everyone with whom we come in contact;
- freedom to encourage, help and allow other associates to grow in knowledge, skill and scope of responsibility;
- the ability to make one's own commitments and keep them;
- consultation with other associates before undertaking actions that could impact the reputation of the company.

With sales of over US $3 billion and 10,000 associates, Gore has appeared in Fortune's annual '100 Best Companies to Work For' list since 1984, ranking seventeenth in 2015, and in the same year was third-placed in the World's Best Multinational Workplaces list by the Great Place to Work® Institute.

Simple processes

'Dunbar's number', together with team size, places limits on the size of an effective operating unit. But being a selling organization is not necessarily about being small per se – it can also be about simple, efficient processes.

Mumbai's dabba (or tiffin) wallas have been the subject of much interest in the world of 'just in time' delivery. Their 125-year-old business model, in which lunchboxes are picked up from a worker's home, delivered to their office and then returned home, still operates with legendary efficiency today. Dabbawallas operate in small teams of up to 25 and have a clearly defined number of lunchboxes to deliver to a very clear and tight timetable. A simple coding system ensures accurate delivery and close customer relationships – dabbawallas are known to their customers personally and cement trust. Despite its reliance on the occasionally erratic Mumbai rail network, the system, which makes 80 million deliveries a year, is so resilient that it has even been claimed to rank as a Six Sigma business. Teamwork and close communication between dabbawallas helps them to make tweaks to deliveries when necessary.

Industrial democracy

Other successful alternative business models have changed the way that decision making happens within organizations. Brazilian manufacturing and services company Semco has been run along unconventional lines by Ricardo Semler since he took it over from his father in the 1980s. Semco operates to three principles: democracy, profit sharing and information. The company uses Dunbar's number, keeping its business units small, but goes beyond structure and team size to change the way that decisions are made: something Semco calls 'participatory management'. Workers are closely involved in many decisions from which they would traditionally be excluded, such as the choice of building. They are strongly empowered to make their own decisions, and (like the dabbawallas) they build up strong relations of trust through their organization. They design their own jobs, decide who will be their manager, and set their own pay and holidays. Semco also created a great deal of internal diversity in skills, so that many of its workers are able to do several different jobs, a move that gave the company strong resilience during Brazil's 1990s downturn.

Like Dee Hock at Visa, Semler aimed to take himself out of the equation – to create an organization that could function without him. This is a radical departure from the cult of the 'hero CEO' that has so recently dominated business.

Lean start-up

This methodology, championed by entrepreneur Eric Ries, turns the traditional approach for starting a business on its head. Conventionally, start-ups begin with a product for which they believe there is a demand. A business plan then follows, along with financial projections, and then financing rounds. Lean start-up starts not by asking the question of whether a product can be built, but whether it *should* be built in the first place: 'Too many start-ups begin with an idea for a product. They then spend months, years, perfecting that product... When they fail to reach broad uptake, it is often because they never spoke to prospective customers. When customers ultimately communicate, through their indifference, that they don't care, the start-up fails.'

Notice one of the lines in Ries's quote? When start-ups fail, it is because they didn't speak to customers or find out whether or not they wanted the new product. The beginning point of the lean start-up methodology builds on the process we have been outlining in this book. It is a simple premise: don't do anything until you really, truly understand what your customers (potential or existing) think and want.

What lean start-up thinks you should do next is to develop a 'build–measure–learn' feedback loop. Once the start-up has identified the problem to be solved, the next step is to develop a minimum viable product (MVP) so this learning process can begin as quickly as possible. This runs counter to the old-fashioned model where monolithic projects are built from the top down – and it looks more like the 'biological' organization depicted in Figure 8.1 than a rigid hierarchy. During the build–measure–learn process, the start-up can tweak the product and be prepared to 'pivot' – change direction or business model – if the learning process suggests that it is necessary.

Dropbox – a lean start-up in action

Lean start-up literature cites file-hosting service Dropbox, which was attempting to break in to the very competitive cloud storage market, as an example of the methodology's success. Dropbox founder Drew Houston's insight was that while there were indeed many products out there, the people he spoke to didn't use them. Using the lean start-up methodology, he created a simple three-minute video as his MVP, publishing it on places like Hacker News and Digg to find out what potential users thought.

Houston notes that this got the same feedback that the Dropbox team would have got had they actually gone ahead and built the product. Then, he and colleagues put up a simple landing page – exemplifying the 'learn early, learn often' approach – and built up a waiting list of 75,000 customers: all this without any actual product development. As Houston points out: 'Not launching is painful, but not learning is fatal... the biggest risk is making something no one wants.' Armed with huge amounts of customer feedback and enthusiasm, Dropbox was able to focus its efforts on 'making an elegant, simple product that just works and makes users happy'. Dropbox users will testify to the simplicity and 'just works' factor that characterizes the product today.

Spotify – new names for new teams

Music streaming service Spotify faces the challenge of many software companies – how to scale and stay agile (in both the traditional and software-development senses of the word) as teams grow internationally. Spotify gets around this problem with an organization comprising squads, tribes, chapters and guilds. A squad is the smallest unit, self-organizing and using lean start-up principles. Tribes are a collection of squads working in a related area – and they also use the Dunbar number to stay at a viable size. Chapters and guilds bind the squads and teams together: chapters comprise people within the same tribe with similar skills, while guilds are broader communities of interest. The company claims that a continuous growth in employee satisfaction has accompanied the introduction of this new system (Kniberg and Ivarsson, 2012).

CASE STUDY   Sonitus Systems – a customer-focused approach to product development

Although it is not a 'lean start-up' example, Futurecurve client Sonitus Systems arrived at a similar way of looking at its go-to-market strategy. Sonitus provides user-friendly and reliable noise-monitoring systems for the global environmental measurement and instrumentation market. The company has achieved continuous sales growth over the last five years and expects sales to double over the next two years as it signs new distributors in Ireland, the UK, Scandinavia and the United States.

Sonitus Managing Director Paul McDonald attributes this growth to the Value Proposition Builder™ process that he encountered.

Paul explained that for Sonitus, its focus on technology was limiting the customers it talked to: 'It is very easy to just talk tech with technical people all day but this means we are often talking to people running very small businesses. They are easy to talk to and to address but they don't scale.' The company's challenge was to find a way to broaden its market into larger and more lucrative organizations.

During a workshop, Paul realized that the Sonitus value proposition was about how its products benefitted customers rather than what the products themselves were capable of: 'I went along thinking that value proposition was something that we would put on the "About Us" page on the website. That is what I had in mind going into it. What stuck with me from the workshop that I still talk to everyone about is that it covered every single touch point of the business and every single customer interaction. That was the biggest takeaway for me.' Paul explained how valuable it was to understand that everything starts with the customer: 'You need to figure out why the customer *would* buy it from you, not why you think the customer *should* buy it from you. And if you don't work that way, someone else will.'

Using the Value Proposition Builder™, Sonitus started to figure out 'why someone thinks we're valuable'. It looked at how it delivered its products, how it talked about them and how it provided after-sales support. Sonitus segmented its existing customers into categories in order to understand in depth what they found valuable about its products – whether it is saving customers time or money, or providing a better service, for example.

Armed with that understanding, the company started to translate this idea of value into everything it does. And once it had packaged its product features in a way that customers found valuable, this gave Sonitus a clear idea of its market position.

There was an immediate impact on one of Sonitus's most important routes to market, as Paul points out: 'When we pushed the new message out to distributors, they "got it" straight away. People who had been struggling with the product got to grips with it and sold it more and more because they now understood how it was valuable to customers.'

Another major change was to cut down the sales cycle, which had previously involved a lengthy process of business travel and face-to-face demonstrations. Sonitus upgraded its website so it became a much more powerful sales channel, moving technical detail into manuals, putting the value upfront and making it easy for customers to navigate.

Sonitus saw immediate benefits from this, as Paul explains:

> Within a week or two we turned around a sale in 24 hours. The customer had visited the new website, done the demo, I could see the feedback coming from the analytics, he got a quote and he said, 'Brilliant, that is what I need', and paid in advance. So we went from very first initial contact to money in the bank in about four days and had a sale agreed in 24 hours.

Overall, Paul describes a 'massive' reduction in sales cycles as Sonitus is now much better prepared to respond to requests for quotes quickly.

The other major benefit of the value proposition work for Sonitus was revenue generation. For example, as Paul explains:

> We closed a deal with a UK company at the start of the year who would have been a major competitor, but as we have refined our products, they have stopped seeing us as a competitor and taken on distribution for us for the whole of the UK. They have helped us to double our revenue from last year already and they recently closed a huge contract as well. We have signed up a few new key distributors and we recently closed a distribution deal to cover all of Scandinavia. We're close to doubling our revenue again in two years.

With a clear story, potential partners can see straight away how Sonitus complements their business.

Sonitus expects to sign a US distributor shortly and has expanded into new premises to deal with its growing customer base. And as it introduces new products, Paul explains that the value proposition approach will continue to be embedded in everything it does: 'We're doing it all again now as we've got a prototype for a new product and we're at the beginning of that process again. I actually went back and read the handbook from the course to make sure we don't get carried away with patting ourselves on the back about our clever technology!'

Clear, open culture

Culture is another route to creating a selling organization, and online shoe retailer Zappos is often held up as an examplar of how company culture drives sales. Now part of Amazon, which bought Zappos in 2009 in a deal reputed to be worth around US $1 billion, Zappos developed 10 core values that it lived by as a company:

- Deliver WOW through service.
- Embrace and drive change.
- Create fun and a little weirdness.
- Be adventurous, creative and open-minded.
- Pursue growth and learning.
- Build open and honest relationships with communication.
- Build a positive team and family spirit.
- Do more with less.
- Be passionate and determined.
- Be humble.

Its recruitment process involved testing cultural fit as well as job suitability, and Zappos focused in particular on creating an excellent customer service experience, for which it became renowned. Under investor and then CEO Tony Hsieh, Zappos hit its target of $1 billion in annual sales two years earlier than planned, and at the time entered the Fortune Top 100 Companies to work for rankings at number 23.

Powerful values and purpose

Consider the average corporate statement of purpose or vision. Here are a few examples of what you might see:

- To maximize shareholder return by delivering premium products and services.
- To be the number one performer in our chosen industries by applying continuous customer focus and process excellence.
- To add value to our stakeholders and markets.
- To satisfy our customers' desires for personal entertainment and information through total customer satisfaction.

It is hard to get motivated by statements like this. They are bland and indistinct, and it's not clear how you as an employee could get personally connected with them. At the time of writing there is great geopolitical upheaval that had at its heart two powerful statements of purpose: 'Vote leave, take control' and 'Make America great again.' In both cases the opposing sides lacked the clear, single-minded unity of purpose and the emotional connection with the people they needed to target.

In business it's the same. When employees are clear about why they turn up for work every day, they are motivated to create a selling organization. America's Southwest Airlines has long been a fixture in the Most Admired and Best to Work For corporate rankings. Its purpose and vision are simple, and powerfully articulated:

- Our purpose: connect people to what's important in their lives through friendly, reliable, low-cost air travel.
- Our vision: to become the World's Most Loved, Most Flown, and Most Profitable Airline.

And the way that Southwest people make this happen is expressed in a set of clear, unique values for employees to live by:

- Warrior spirit.
- Servant's heart.
- Fun-LUVing attitude.
- Work the Southwest way.

Southwest is famed for its singing and rapping flight attendants, humorous safety briefings and countless stories of staff 'going the extra mile' for customers. Its values are so effective because they are grounded in a strong, meaningful purpose and vision.

In contrast with many corporate vision and mission statements, Southwest's are clear and genuinely differentiating. More importantly, they are connected directly to Southwest's customers and what they want from air travel – which is not necessarily the experience of flying but the value of being 'connected to what's important in their lives'. Today, Southwest carries the most domestic passengers of any US airline, employs over 52,000 people and, in 2015, made profits of over $2 billion.

What next?

We have looked at several different ways of creating the 'selling organization':

- small, semi-autonomous teams;
- decentralized organizations;
- simple processes;
- industrial democracy;
- lean start-up;
- clear, open culture;
- powerful values and purpose.

In all the cases we have reviewed, the organizations in question had clear value propositions and clear ways to translate them into sales propositions. But they have all illustrated that to do this successfully – and to become a genuinely customer-driven organization – the traditional command-and-control hierarchical company structure doesn't cut it. In the selling organization, everyone's work is tilted towards the customer.

From Southwest's cabin attendants to Gore's Associates to Spotify's Guilds, people in these successful companies are all, in effect, selling while they work. And like in Giles Hutchins's visualization of the resilient organizational form, these companies are all better designed to resist the constant change that is an unavoidable feature of the commercial world. In organizations like these, 'change management' ought to be a redundant discipline, because they manage change by default – thanks to features like good communication, mutual trust and strong feedback loops.

The type of selling organization you choose to be will depend on many different variables: your prevailing culture, the size and age of the business, the industry you're in, the technology you use and the people you employ. But the examples we have used show what is possible.

There has been lots to think about and action in this book; however, make sure you follow Law 7.

> 7th Law of Value Proposition Selling: don't try to change everything all at once; you will need an evolutionary plan.

For many organizations this process has been the start of a transformation, often a transformation from a product-centric organization to a much more customer-centric one. This has many implications and requires a considered strategy and plan over several years.

> 10th Law of Value Proposition Selling: this process – the value proposition work and organizational adjustments – never stops.

To keep pace with your customers and market changes, this process needs to be built into an organization's internal culture and all aspects of regular operation. Many of the organizations we have featured in this book created a value proposition function to ensure this became an ongoing process. The longer-term rewards of this will speak for themselves.

We wish you every success.

References

Cook, Peter (2016) *Leading Innovation, Creativity and Enterprise*, Bloomsbury Information Ltd, an imprint of Bloomsbury Publishing Plc, London

Hutchins, Giles (2016a) [accessed 13 January 2017] Redesigning for Resilience [Blog] *Human Spaces* [Online] http://humanspaces. com/2016/08/29/the-future-of-business-redesigning-for-resilience/

Hutchins, Giles (2016b) [accessed 13 January 2017] The Evolution of the Living Organization [Blog] *The Nature of Business* [Online] https://thenatureofbusiness.org/2016/10/24/ the-evolution-of-the-living-organization/#more-1506

Hutchins, Giles (2016c) *Future Fit*, Amazon, US

Kniberg, Henrik and Ivarsson, Anders (2012) [accessed 13 January 2017] Scaling Agile@Spotify with Tribes, Squads, Chapters & Guilds [Online] https://www.scribd.com/document/113617905/Scaling-Agile-Spotify?ad_group=Online+Tracking+Link&campaign=Skimbit%2C+ Ltd.&content=10079&irgwc=1&keyword=ft500noi&medium=affiliate &source=impactradius

Ludvigsen, Karl (2009) [accessed 13 January 2017] Not So Sclerotic: The Truth About General Motors, *The Spectator* [Online] http://www.spectator.co.uk/2009/12/not-so-sclerotic-the-truth-about-general-motors/

Ries, Eric [accessed 13 January 2017] The Lean Startup Methodology, *The Lean Startup* [Online] http://theleanstartup.com/principles

Ries, Eric [accessed 13 January 2017] The Lean Startup [Online] http:// theleanstartup.com/casestudies#dropbox

Southwest Airlines [accessed 13 January 2017] [Online] https://www. southwest.com/html/about-southwest/careers/culture.html

Waldrop, M Mitchell (1996) [accessed 13 January 2017] The Trillion-Dollar Vision of Dee Hock [Blog] *Fast Company* [Online] https:// www.fastcompany.com/27333/trillion-dollar-vision-dee-hockZappos [accessed 13 January 2017] [Online] Zappos.com/core-values

APPENDIX 1
Value Proposition Workshop survey results

Many companies participated in a series of workshops using the Value Proposition Builder™ methodology. These companies ranged from technology and industrials to logistics providers, and they were coached to learn and then apply the methodology in their own businesses.

In the context of this book, the workshops essentially followed the steps described in Chapter 3, 'How to develop a value proposition'.

The businesses involved in this survey were mostly small to medium-sized enterprises (SMEs).

Figure App 1.1 Breakdown of delegate companies by turnover and payroll

Revenues

Less than €1m		20.0%
Between €1m and €10m		52.0%
More than €10m		28.0%

Employees

0 – 10 employees		20.0%
10 – 100 employees		56.0%
More than 100 employees		24.0%

Reasons for enrolling

This was an optional workshop for businesses, which enrolled on it for a variety of reasons:

- expand into new markets, including overseas;
- improve the customer offer;
- understand the customer offer;
- convey a technical message to investors.

Key challenges cited by delegates included, in rank order:

- lack of growth, either revenue or sales;
- being driven towards commodity price strategies;
- promotions and communication efforts not engaging target audiences effectively;
- cost-cutting and lean efficiencies have been achieved;
- competitors are taking the lead in their markets.

Working with the Value Proposition Builder™ process

We asked delegates to describe the experience of working with the Value Proposition Builder™ process:

Figure App 1.2   Delegates' experience of working with the Value Proposition Builder™ process

'Really forced deep dive analysis and helped us to formulate and then in turn articulate our proposition in a way that could be communicated to and from all levels within the company.'

'Great for gaining insights into where the customer sees us bringing value. Validates the things we do well. Informs us as to where we need to improve.'

'It helped cement a belief that we already had but were unable to successfully deliver/promote to our clients. It also made us realize that certain segments of our target industry are best left to the opposition.'

'The course gave me a really practical tool kit to support the development of a new sales strategy for the business.'

(Continued)

Figure App 1.2 *(Continued)*

'It provides a language and structure to use when presenting our business. When building a new business (or working in an existing business) one is very close to it and it can be hard to step back and put key elements into a framework that others (potential clients and/or investors) can understand in a succinct and clear manner.'

'The workshop provided an excellent 'out of the office' forum for our team to discuss and analyse our offering to the market in a structured and focused fashion. Oftentimes these important concepts and exercises are avoided by small companies as they are considered too complex to tackle but the Futurecurve approach makes it not only achievable in a short time frame but also in a fun and instructive way.'

'A very valuable exercise that achieved our aim of identifying our value drivers to communicate with investors but also enabled the company to focus on customers needs better.'

'Our business is all about identifying value for our customers – the tool is perfect for this. We then put our efforts into developing the capability to create more value and of course to eliminate waste.

'It was a systematic process where each step in the builder built upon the last. This was something that we could replicate outside of the programme for our different offerings.'

How the businesses have implemented what they learned

Twelve months after the workshop, we contacted businesses to understand how, if at all, they had put what they had learned into practice.

Figure App 1.3 confirms that while the most popular approach was to feed the value proposition work through to marketing messages, over half of delegate businesses had also gone on to repeat the process internally. Nearly half had 'reset' their company vision and over one-third had changed the products and services they sold.

Figure App 1.3   How delegates have implemented what they learned

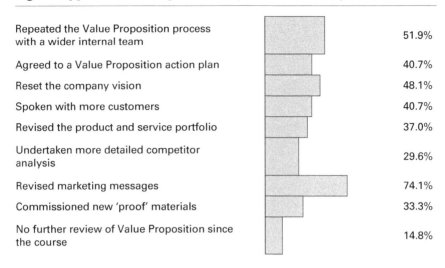

Repeated the Value Proposition process with a wider internal team	51.9%
Agreed to a Value Proposition action plan	40.7%
Reset the company vision	48.1%
Spoken with more customers	40.7%
Revised the product and service portfolio	37.0%
Undertaken more detailed competitor analysis	29.6%
Revised marketing messages	74.1%
Commissioned new 'proof' materials	33.3%
No further review of Value Proposition since the course	14.8%

Barriers to implementation

While none of the businesses had any problem getting management buy-in, one-third cited lack of resources for an implementation programme as a barrier to putting the workshop into practice. The most common problem, however, was the simple fact of being too busy: nearly 60 per cent of respondents were held back by operational business pressures from putting their plans into practice:

Figure App 1.4   Barriers to implementation

Lack of senior management commitment to drive the Value Proposition through	3.7%	1
Unable to fund the required change	7.4%	2
No management buy-in to adopt the Value Proposition and the implementation programme	0.0%	0
Do not have the skills to implement the Value Proposition work	11.1%	3
Lack of resources for an implementation programme	29.6%	8
Operational business pressures mean there is no time for implementation	59.3%	16
Not confident that the organization can deliver/achieve the desired change	11.1%	3

Results and successes

Following the workshops nearly half of the businesses that attended went on to create a new value proposition for their businesses; and over 73 per cent continue to use the Value Proposition Builder™ today.

When asked what success the methodology had achieved for them, responses range from an improved understanding of the business's value to measurable financial improvement (see Figure App 1.5):

Figure App 1.5 Measurable improvement after adopting the Value Proposition Builder™ methodology

'A fuller pipeline.'

'Sales cycles have been cut from months to days, we have targeted messages for each customer segment, clear strategies on how to find new customers and distributors. Sales have doubled each year and our ability to serve those customers has been streamlined by the clarity of our own offering.'

'Clearer more concise value proposition. Understood by all.'

'We have a much better understanding of where we are going, we are on track and slowly transitioning our client base, our engagements and are focused on "demonstrating" the results of our capability. We had ignored the evidence of our successes that is right under our noses.'

'Clarity.'

'The process has been used as part of the strategic growth plan for the company. Evidence of its success is that growth targets are being achieved year on year since implementation.'

'We identified that having closer engagement with our customers by making our scientists available to advise and visit more was a hidden customer need we were fulfilling. By increasing these interactions we have increased sales, especially repeat ones, but also gained new insights into applications for our technology.'

'We have grown from €15 million to €40 million. Obviously this is not all because of the builder but it certainly helps.'

'The process directed us towards a change in our market targeting.'

'It has allowed us to measure our success and progress in a more systematic and considered way. It gives us common language to analyse performance and interpret market behaviours.'

'Helped us to focus on customer needs and on packaging of our product.'

APPENDIX 2
Case studies

Context

Thermodial is a building services engineering company providing planned preventative maintenance services for heating, ventilation, air conditioning, building management systems, electrical and water services.

Andy Donlan, Marketing Manager Thermodial, told us:

Together with one of our directors I attended a Value Proposition Builder™ workshop, which introduced us to the formal concept of value proposition. I think both of us walking out of that one-day workshop were actually quite excited about the prospect of what the Value Proposition Builder™ could do for the business. It is a systematic process where each step in the builder builds upon the last and this was something that we felt suited our business processes and could be replicated internally.

Challenge

Our overall goal is to get the conversation away from price and more towards other value elements of our service – and if you can be on-message with what you're saying there, then you can steer the conversation away from price alone. Obviously there is a cost to everything, we understand that, but we want to exhibit some of the other benefits to our service as well.

Action

We have approached our value proposition through a sector at a time as we are active in seven business sectors. For example, hospitals is one of our sectors – we will look at that and do a value proposition workshop with some of our staff internally to find out what it is that customers value. I will have done my own research and interviewed a selection of customers in that sector and I will bring that into the workshop. We go through Futurecurve's

Value Proposition Builder™, the six stages, and finish with something that is twofold: one, we end up with something that we need, especially when we are looking for new customers; two, we also engage with our staff, which involves them in the decision making of the business – this is part of our ethos. Everyone contributes; our people are very clued-in and hands on – and when you put them in a team environment and don't disregard any ideas, we really get something of value out of the process at the end of it, I think. You need a certain number of people, obviously. We found that about five or six people in the team – from different departments – is ideal.

We now have a more systemized process to gathering customer feedback; I have a template for testimonials, which enables us to get the best messages from customers. Generally there is far more awareness around the company from the managers and the directors; they are tipping me off on specific projects, 'We've done a specific energy-saving project there. Maybe you should talk to the person responsible and write it up.' Or 'I think that might form part of a value statement.' We add the customer testimonials to our website, which helps us in the future when we are going for more customers in that sector.

We have a display system in the office that holds the main points of the value proposition statement from each specific sector. We put the system on the wall so it is visible for everyone to see. It all works very well but you need to have someone like me implementing it day-to-day and I need to have the support of the board, which I have – that is exactly what you need.

Results

What it has done is that it has given our people more confidence going into sales situations with people they haven't met before as we are absolutely on message then with what those people want to hear in any given sector. So it does give a lot of confidence when going into meetings.

Learning

The value proposition process has given us structure; it has meant that we have a template for each of the sectors that we are operating in. I would definitely build in some implementation time, to work on your post-statement plan if you want to call it that… You cannot just do it and let it fall by the wayside.

I would say that getting people involved from different parts of the business definitely helped us because some of the things that have come out of the workshops are things that neither the management nor I could have come up with, as these are the people who are facing the customer day-to-day – so that information is gold!

Future

There are common themes emerging from our sector work that I am now analysing for our overall company value proposition statement, but I have yet to sit down and formalize that.

CASE STUDY CCN

Computational Class Notes (CCN) is a self-funded start-up with a vision to enable easy access to education. Based on advanced computational technology, CCN has developed a cloud-based educational platform that can take a wide range of materials from university or college professors, including class notes, reference materials, practice worksheets, etc, and make them available to students via their smartphones and other mobile devices. This accessibility results in increased student learning, success and grades, lower dropout rates, and better use of professorial time to spend in creative work, research and writing, which is vital to the professor and the institution.

Delivering a real-time, dynamic learning environment for both professors and students significantly overcomes some of the organizational and financial barriers inhibiting the education sector.

Director Lucia Valente told us:

We are a start-up, we are not a mature company and we will continue to evolve. We are passionate educators; we want to make a difference to education. If what we are doing does not enhance student learning or help them master their subject or build confidence in what they are doing, resulting in enhanced learning and grades, then we are not going to do it. Our technology, the algorithms we have developed, can be applied to a spectrum of other areas but we have chosen education because that is what we believe in. We are targeting professors because they are the decision makers, they give us the entré to the university or college – the ultimate customer is the student.

Context

We are still educating students using a 19th-century model. We should be thinking about the future; what education model does the 21st century require? It is not the same education I experienced – the current education model still thinks in terms of the 19th century model, so what we have tried to do is shake this up and say, 'We want to look and think about education for the future' – that's why I called our service *The Modern Professor*; to reflect the concept of changing the way we are imparting knowledge. The key thing is that we deliver very dynamic learning, unlimited practice questions with quizzes and other tools, bringing the content to life while remaining highly interactive and adaptive to the student, which is dramatically different to learning with passive books and material.

We provide the technology platform and then help the professor to put all their course materials online. It is the professor's material and class notes. The professor has shaped it and their picture is placed on the course modules and content – the class notes. They are the authors and their name is placed prominently on all class materials. Professors are not only delivering a course (and they take pride in that) – they are intimately involved in the development of the class modules. We work collaboratively and iteratively with each professor – it is their class content running on our technology. We help them to deliver their knowledge digitally to become *The Modern Professor*, to enhance their students' learning, retention and mastery as well as returning valuable time into their schedules.

Challenge

Education is more than just getting grades, it is about 'learning' and that is the trap that educational institutions have run into: the student wants the grade, they don't care if they have learnt the subject matter or not. This is the problem that education is now facing. We have read so many articles and I have watched so many YouTube videos about students who graduate with good grades but when they are put into the real world they haven't learned how to problem-solve – and that goes right back to students saying, 'I just want to get a grade, I just want to pass', but that is not education and that is not knowledge.

For many students that pressure for success is increased by their financial situation. Professors we work with tell us that some of their students are so poor that if they have to buy a book that costs $50 or $100 this could mean that month that they have very little money for food. That's wrong. In this day and age that is wrong and we feel very passionately about making education affordable for students who want to learn; our mission is removing barriers to learning and this is what we are focusing on at CCN.

Action

The Value Proposition Builder™ encourages engagement with the customer – and that has really influenced how we approach our development process when our developers engage with our professors. Our product is software, our company is virtual and we are dealing with customers all over the United States. We have a forum where we talk to our customers and we are now putting a lot of effort and thought into our development site. That is something very tangible that we did and the professors love it, because we have given them a voice in this process.

I would say that the Value Proposition Builder™ confirmed our understanding of who our client is and how we deliver our messaging; it has helped us to really hone that. This was one of the things we were struggling with, because we have developed very advanced technology and when you are working so close to it, delivering an appropriate and targeted message so that people really understand what you're doing – and trying to get the language appropriate for the customer – really challenged me. I am now crisper in my messaging and I have more confidence now when I'm reaching out to a new professor.

Results

We found that the process provided a language and structure to use when presenting our business. When building a new business one is very close to it and it can be hard to step back and put key elements into a framework that others, potential clients and/or investors, can understand in a succinct and clear manner.

The success that we have achieved is with the actual language in our presentations and in our discussions with potential clients. Framing the context of our product to our market is more clear and succinct. As a start-up, our market messaging is an ongoing process of improvement and enhancement.

Learning

One of our key learnings using the Value Pyramid™ has been how to price the product or service. Our product is very, very sophisticated and it should be priced in a certain way, but because we are at the early stages of our business development we are pricing it transactionally, so we know there is a slight disconnect between our value and price. Right now we are dealing with individual professors because this is how we are growing our business and we price at a per-student payment; I am actually very comfortable with that model but I do know that eventually the buyer will shift to the university (and not the individual professor) and they will buy/pay for the service. We have had a breakthrough at one of the universities in Canada where one of the professors received funding from the dean of the college and we are now getting a lump sum from them. We will see how that evolves as we anticipate two pricing models, two options in our proposals. One thing that we really learnt from the course and are now aware of is that our positioning, the sophistication of our product and its value must be aligned.

CASE STUDY Abcon

Context

Abcon Industrial Products Ltd is an engineering manufacturing company specializing in abrasives and it is the only Irish manufacturer of abrasive belts and quick-change discs. Serving a wide range of industries, including automotive, stainless steel fabricators, aircraft maintenance, oil and gas exploration and mining and aggregate producers, the product range spans cutting, sanding, painting and finishing products, which are supplied to domestic and international markets. The company has achieved sales growth continuously over the last five years.

Director Barry Smith told us:

> The Value Proposition Builder™ process forced us to make a deep-dive analysis and helped us to formulate and then articulate the Abcon value in a way that could be communicated to and from all levels within the company. The value proposition approach was the basis of our strategic growth plan and our growth targets are being achieved year on year since its implementation.

Challenge

Sales and Marketing Director, Lyn Sharkey continued:

> We have a really wide range of products and when we carried out the Value Pyramid™ exercise and looked at what our core products are, it definitely helped us to focus and we did a lot of work around that. The ongoing challenge is to maintain the focus while carrying out basic everyday

functions. You need to be conscious that it is something that you need to do continuously, not just on a one-off basis, but transform it into a behaviour that you are living with every day, even when things get busy, and obviously it is not the most urgent thing on your list!

Action

Instead of spending time trying to compose a sales message that fit the company as a whole, we realized that actually we have different customer segments, and the sales proposition is different for each of those, so I think that was definitely learning for us.

Results

We used the Value Proposition Builder™ as the basis for developing our strategic growth plan, but I think it has been even more useful than that. I believe that it can actually help you during decision-making processes. If you are considering a new product, for example, or making decisions regarding the direction your growth might take, you know that you are maintaining your core values if you go back to the value proposition work and check if your decision is in line with that. That alignment – to have that framework and to be able to go back to and refer to it – is great because things move on so quickly and you get pulled in all sorts of directions. Our nature as a business is not to let opportunities go by, but maybe we shouldn't take every opportunity that comes along either, we need to have some base to go back to, to decide if that opportunity is for us or not.

Learning

Every company needs some guidance and help on 'How do we get to the core of what we do?' Your core value is likely to be common across your business, even if your range is diverse. We were originally thinking about our sales tag lines, but I think that the Value Proposition Builder™ approach has helped enable us really to understand what is of value for our customers and has given us structure and a framework that we can use to understand what our value is and how it can help us.

Everyone should consider how to apply it to the day-to-day business because it can help you with your decision making. The learning we gained from that, having done the work, is that it can help you to make your business decisions more clearly.

CASE STUDY Geoscience Ireland

Context

Geoscience Ireland is a membership organization representing a network of companies delivering design, consultancy and contracting services through their geological expertise. Members work in a range of extractive and infrastructure industries, including water services, minerals exploration and mining, environmental and geotechnical engineering and infrastructure development. With clients in over 50 countries, the network is supported by Irish government bodies: the Geological Survey Ireland and Enterprise Ireland.

Over a four-year period the network has grown to more than 28 members, who collaborate with each other and with related academic and research institutions, to win and deliver significant international geoscience projects.

Sean Finlay, Director, and Andrew Gaynor, Business Development Executive, told us:

> Our growing members are all in the geoscience sector; we have skills ranging from civil engineers to environmental consultants, so there are probably three or four different groupings. At the moment we are made up of largely SMEs, the largest of which would be about 250 people. In addition to having consultants we also have contractors. Consultants and contractors operate in the same sectors but do business differently.

Challenge

> We are not a legal entity because we are a government-supported programme so our role is to assist members to collaborate, identify and submit proposals for geoscience project and contracts. As part of our service to them we examine a number of tendering portals every week to identify and circulate opportunities. We try to matchmake members, encouraging them to pursue appropriate tender opportunities.

Action

> When we first adopted the Value Proposition Builder™ process I think we had five members; now we have 28. The process helped us with our vision, our value proposition and the physical outputs of that. It is a thought-provoking process that has provided direction for us and it has also been useful for ongoing engagement with stakeholders.

We agreed on our value proposition and have refined it on two occasions, as we have repeated the Value Proposition Builder™ process. We find that having this conversation with the members at a workshop is a great way to get them talking and collaborating and interacting with one another. We discuss with each other the vision and outlook for the next six or twelve months in order to check that it loosely aligns with the new value proposition we have. It is a useful benchmark for the future.

Results

Not being a private company we don't have sales and cost-reduction targets or anything like that; our metrics are around how the companies are doing, how many members we have, how many net new jobs they create. What we are interested in is job creation and economic growth. Our members are interested in developing themselves as companies and winning more contracts – that is the value-add we are looking to provide. We get great feedback from them – so that is a metric in itself.

Learning

Our learning advances through the willingness to keep looking at our value proposition and to challenge it, and to keep asking one another the relevant questions and to come to it with an open mind, to try to widen the consultee field, get as many network members as possible involved in the process. The underlying message is there, members share that and are working together towards the long-term vision – and the fact that most of the members were involved in the value proposition consultation process gives us stakeholder buy-in. It actually does improve communication and collaboration between people; it is a great tool in that regard.

Future

We are at a bit of a crossroads in that we are likely to try to attract the larger companies to become members. Typically there will be three prongs to a business cluster: you will have tier-one multinationals, you will have SMEs and you will have a very strong research and development – an innovation element as well. We have good strong links to academic research and with SMEs but we don't have the first part, the larger indigenous consultants and contractors – but that is our ambition.

To achieve this I think we will need to augment our value proposition strategy because the larger companies will probably take the view that as they are large, why would they bother joining. What's in it for them?

CASE STUDY Biocel

Context

Biocel Ltd is an industrial chemicals company, manufacturing and supplying high-quality, specialist chemical formulations to a variety of markets, including food and drink, laundry and water treatment in both private and public sectors. The company was not realizing its potential as fast as the senior management team would like.

Technical Sales Manager Dr Karl McCarthy told us:

> We are an industrial market company and, from experience with our buyers, it is very much a case of, 'Well show me that it does what it says on the tin!' It is about performance, targeted performance.

> What made a fundamental difference to our value proposition journey was to realize that if we are to export to either large national or multinational companies, we will only be successful in a foreign market if we can deliver on something that no one else could. We would have to identify a very high value product or a very high value service that we could deliver on, and using the Value Pyramid™ was very insightful and helped us to realize that. We needed more clarity on that, we should have realized that earlier on – it seems obvious, but it was very insightful, so we put a lot of focus and energy into trying to identify those elements. It's clarity you need and I suppose the clarity comes with the data, but in this day and age there is so much data, there are so many experts – to get that crystallization really helped us to define the route ahead.

Challenge

> We want to get to a situation where we can design and deliver product. We are good at the service aspect of it but that's very difficult to export. In our industry, here in Ireland, you do have to send a person out, as that personal level of service is expected by customers and then you gain their trust and can partner with them: to generate trust and generate business – it is very hands-on.

Action

> We put a focus on R&D and reimagined our company as a bespoke industrial performance chemical company. Our clients are primarily in the food and beverage industry. They have particular problems and they come to us

for help and advice. We spend a lot of time designing targeted solutions, bespoke products. We realize that while that is very good on the ground, in a national sense, if we are to identify an exportable product we would have to do some fundamental R&D and design a product using our particular skill set that is exportable, marketable and scalable. Our customers expect that personal bespoke service, so the question is how do we blend a product and consultancy service?

I'm going out to Asia this weekend doing that very job; one of our large customers contacted us via their Irish headquarters, and I spoke to their technical guy out there and he said, 'Look, we have problems here, can you come out and help us?' I'm going to spend a week helping and advising them, so there is that consultancy aspect. We've got a consulting service, so it is really taking that Value Pyramid™ and looking at the 'co-created' element, and then all our products will trickle down from that.

Results

We were on a client site the other day where we did some very quick calculations and made some very simple adjustments that could save them a six-figure sum per year. So it is that kind of stuff; we said, 'If you do this, this and this, you will save so much.' Having that knowledge is absolutely what we are about and it plays directly into improving performance. It's great that we have identified the core of what our value is. I always tell people that my job description is turning ideas into invoices!

Learnings

Our experience has been that once you have identified the route to market, you have to go and do it. From experience you can get distracted from the core task of identifying and meeting customer needs. The Value Pyramid™ has really helped me with that. You have got to be confident about what you are going for but don't get bogged down in the process.

ABOUT THE AUTHORS

Our core beliefs

We are led by an unshakeable belief: that if we understand our rational, emotional and social interactions in business better, we know our companies, ourselves, our employees, our customers and our suppliers better. This builds stronger relationships and better performance.

We believe that business is a force for good and that our approach can help business address the most important challenges of our time.

Cindy Barnes

As the founder and Chief Innovation Officer of Futurecurve, Cindy's passion for genuine customer-centricity in business is transforming the operations and perspective of major companies around the world.

Beginning her career in engineering, she transitioned to running large-scale unionized factories for Smiths Industries. Later, leading R&D for part of Panavision, she developed a cutting-edge technical product range (still their most profitable to date). Cindy led service development, sales and marketing for Capgemini, where she initiated their first service offering and established a business unit that generated £100m in sales during its first year.

Cindy holds an MBA and has qualifications in engineering, physics, operations management and psychology. Her studies in psychology inform the work of Futurecurve, and she is a member of the British Association of Counselling and Psychotherapy and the British Psychological Society.

She is co-author of the best-selling business book *Creating and Delivering Your Value Proposition*.

Helen Blake

During her 25-year career as an experienced sales and marketing professional, Helen held senior positions in prominent businesses around the world, including Accenture, KPMG and Capgemini. In these roles, Helen's passionate advocacy for including the customer as a central participant in business identity has been pivotal in catalysing growth, efficiency and success.

For the last 10 years, Helen has been the Chief Executive of Futurecurve, the leading value proposition and customer-centricity consultancy, where she demonstrates the power and profitability of integrity in business. Helen's success in implementing growth strategies for Fortune 500 companies, start-ups, governmental organizations and not-for-profits continues to validate the benefits of integrity in all aspects of operation.

She speaks extensively on the subject of value propositions and is co-author of the business best-seller *Creating and Delivering Your Value Proposition*.

In addition to being a leading business professional, Helen is trained in organizational psychology and is a member of the International Transactional Analysis Association. She also holds various marketing qualifications, is an alumna of Stanford GSB, and is a Fellow of the Royal Society of Arts.

Tamara Howard

Tamara is the co-founder of Verve Consulting, providing strategic business development expertise to technology and life science sectors. She earned her AB at Harvard, a PhD from Sackler School of Biomedical Sciences, Tufts University, and is a trustee and director of the Harvard Club of the UK.

During her 35 years of experience in multinational sales and marketing positions at Bethesda Research Labs, IBM, PA Consulting, Digital, and as a divisional director for Capgemini, Tamara developed and implemented highly effective methods to help international teams deliver on business goals.

Tamara is the author of *Who's Paying for Lunch? – A practical manual for maximizing sales in small and medium enterprises, Putting the Soul Back into Business – A roadmap of social change,* and *100+ Top Tips for Effective Sales Management.*

INDEX

Note: The index is filed in alphabetical, word-by-word order. Numbers within main headings and 'Mc' are filed as spelt out. Acronyms are filed as presented. Page locators in *italics* denote information contained within a Figure or Table.